I0123369

Bar Stories

Famous Bars with Stories to Tell

Terry W. Lyons

Copyright © 2024 Terry W. Lyons
ISBN: 978-1-970153-48-4
Distributed by Ingram Book Company

Cover Photo
Sean Ryan Pub
2019 14th Ave, Vero Beach, FL 32960

No part of this publication may be reproduced or transmitted in any form or by any means, graphic, electronic, photocopy, recording, or by any information storage retrieval system — except for excerpts used for published review — without the written permission of the Author.

Maison

La Maison Publishing
Vero Beach, Florida
The Hibiscus City
lamaisonpublishing@gmail.com

Table of Contents

INTRODUCTION

This book describes drinking establishments around the world where famous people have gathered and significant incidents occurred. There are over fifty separate short stories, and in almost all cases, the places are still there and open for business. You can still go into the Grenadier Pub in London, sit down, and have a drink in the same spot where the Duke of Marlborough and his officers celebrated the defeat of Napoleon just across the English Channel at the battle of Waterloo in 1815. You can go to the Top of the Mark lounge at the Mark Hopkins hotel in San Francisco, sit in the same corner, known as the "weeping corner," have a drink or a meal, and watch ships leave for the Pacific Ocean and ports in the Far East.

This is the very same table in the very same corner where, eighty years ago, mothers, young wives, and friends sat watching their loved ones depart to fight the Japanese in World War II.

On a brighter note, I describe the Carousel Bar at the Hotel Monteleone in New Orleans, usually considered America's most famous and most favorite drinking spot. This is the bar that looks like a carousel and revolves just like a carousel. The list of celebrities, especially authors, who have enjoyed drinking here is lengthy. These are a few of the places covered in this book. These are all places that are still open daily for business, and most haven't changed very much despite operating, in some cases, for hundreds of years.

I hope you find both enjoyment and enrichment in these stories. Close your eyes for a few minutes and imagine what it was like for these people celebrating or mourning, plotting, or just listening in these places. Patrons include everyone from Al Capone running his criminal empire from the Green Mill saloon in Chicago to the Cavendish laboratory scientist announcing the discovery of DNA at the 400-year-old Eagle Pub on the campus of Cambridge University, still open and serving food and drinks every day.

There is a table and chair at the end of the bar in the Menger hotel in San Antonio, TX. Back in 1898, Teddy Roosevelt sat at this same table and chair, recruiting men for his Rough Riders, who later stormed San Juan Hill in the Spanish-American war.

It was necessary to include a couple of restored Taverns in order to describe places that played such an important role in the American Revolution. Daniel Webster called the Tavern the "birthplace of the American Revolution." The Tavern served every purpose, from plotting the uprising to serving as a hospital once the fighting began. The American Taverns in this book are exact replicas and are in daily operation, providing drinks and snacks that are typical of the Revolutionary Period.

One chapter is devoted to my own true personal collection of bar stories. Growing up in Olean, New York, population 21,000, in the 40s and 50s, I attended public school #2. We walked to school every morning, walked to and from school for lunchtime, and returned home at 3:00 PM. The grade school was located on State Street, one of the main streets in the town. It was about three short blocks from my house, and on this trip, four times a day for eight years, I passed three average-sized bars. All three were typical American bars of the period. The front had two entrances. One led directly into the bar, and the other opened to the dining area. The bar names were the Cabin, the Silver Slipper, and the Wagon Wheel.

The Cabin was the worst appearing of the trio, and it happened to be on my side of the busy street. We were not allowed to cross the street until we reached the school, where there was a traffic light and a policeman.

Weather permitting, the bar side door of the Cabin was always wide open, and you got a very strong odor of stale beer. A large Saint Bernard dog always stood on the top step, usually asleep because the customers gave him plenty of beer.

By the time I was seventeen years old and a junior in high school, we began to hang out at the Wagon Wheel bar. The New York State drinking age was eighteen, but the owner let us drink beer as long as we stayed on the dining side; we were not allowed in the bar area. This was a good arrangement, especially in the winter months when Olean, New York, is a very cold and snowy place. The dining room had a regular original hardwood surface shuffleboard game, and some of our group became experts at the sport.

I often think that this early exposure to bars may have led to my lifelong interest and fascination with them. Of course, it probably helped that I am Irish.

Following high school, four years at Purdue University in West Lafayette, IN, removed me from the bar scene for a while. Unlike New York State, the drinking age in Indiana was 21, and believe me, they were anxious to enforce it. Gambling and prostitution didn't seem to be a problem, but if caught drinking, you were expelled from school.

Once I completed college and Army Service and embarked on a career in sales, marketing, and advertising with Eastman Kodak, I resumed my interest in bars.

I've selected about a dozen stories that actually took place while I was having a drink or a meal alone or with friends in a bar. Most of these stories are humorous, all have good outcomes, and everything takes place in a bar.

Finally, I've included many favorite bar jokes that I have collected over my years of participating in the bar scene.

You will notice frequent mention of Winston Churchill and Ernest Hemingway throughout the book. Churchill, often considered the greatest figure of the 20th century, was renowned for his heavy consumption of a variety of alcoholic beverages. He appears in this book because of his sparkling wit and wisdom relating to drinking alcohol. Ernest Hemingway was a reporter and a journalist, and this resulted in living for extended periods in five separate countries. Somehow, his drinking skills left an indelible mark on the bar scene in every one of the countries. In France, even today, the Hemingway bar is a major attraction in Paris. He didn't just appear and have a drink in all these places; he left a memory and a story, and he was actually in the bar daily, drinking serving as a facilitator of his writing.

As Churchill said, "I've taken more out of alcohol than alcohol has taken out of me."

Alcohol is the subject because no great story ever started over a salad.

Weepers Corner. Top of the Mark Hopkins Hotel

Carousel Lounge, Monteleone Hotel, New Orleans

Earnest Hemmingway

Sloppy Joe's, Key West

Algonquin-Round-Table #5

Dorothy Parker

Green Mill Lounge, Chicago

Al Capone

Menger Hotel Bar, San Antonio

Teddy Roosevelt and the Rough Riders

Pump Room, Ambassador East Hotel

Harry Caray, Baseball Announcer

Anchor Bar, Buffalo, NY

Billy Bob's, Ft. Worth, TX

Stonewall Inn, New York City

King Cole Bar, St. Regis

Bemelmans Bar, Historic Hotel Carlyle

Bemelmans, Carlyle Hotel, NYC

Yankee Doodle Bar Mural

Nassau Inn, Princeton, NJ

Booth #2, Pete's Tavern, New York City

Brunswick Bar, The Palace Saloon, Prescott, AZ

Talbott Tavern, Bardstown, Ky

CHAPTER 1

The Top of the Mark Bar is located on the 19th floor of the Mark Hopkins hotel on Nob Hill at the corner of California and Mason streets in downtown San Francisco. It sits atop the highest spot in San Francisco, and on a fog- free day, with its 360-degree view, you can see the Golden Gate Bridge, Chinatown, the Bay, and North Beach.

The Mark Hopkins Hotel was built in 1926 and included an eleven-room penthouse suite on the 19th floor, leased to Daniel Jackson for the 1923 equivalent of $21,000 a month. Jackson managed to live there in the penthouse for ten years. In 1936, the hotel decided to convert the penthouse into a glass-walled cocktail lounge, which became known as the Top of the Mark. In the 1940s, radio KSFO began broadcasting celebrity interviews nightly from the bar, and it became well known.

During World War II, 1941- 1945, San Francisco was the major transit point for troops departing for the Pacific theater. Service men started a tradition of having a farewell drink at the Top of the Mark and a final dance before shipping out to fight in the war. At the time, Life magazine published an article that claimed over

30,000 servicemen took the Mark Hopkins hotel elevator to the Top of the Mark every month.

The northwest corner of the bar, with its view of the Golden Gate Bridge, became known as "weepers' corner," named for the wives, mothers, and girlfriends who would gather there for one final look at the departing warships with their loved ones on board. Just try to imagine the memories that corner of the room holds, some so sad and others full of joy.

I have a personal story concerning the Top of the Mark bar. My oldest brother joined the Army Air Force (there was no separate Air Force branch) after high school at eighteen years old. He became a B17 and B25 bomber pilot stationed at an air base in Nevada. We received a letter from him containing a postcard photo of the Top of the Mark. The letter described the big evening they had at the famous bar celebrating the unit's preparation to depart for the Pacific. Well, I can still remember my mother going to her very own "weeper's corner." Other events prevailed, and the squadron did not depart for the Far East. Thank God.

The Korean War, 1950- 1953, started another tradition at the Top of the Mark bar. Squadrons of airmen preparing to depart for Korea would purchase a bottle of whiskey to be kept available at the bar, known as the "squadron bottle." Each member of the squadron would sign and date the label whenever he stopped by and had a free drink. The man who had the last drink would keep the empty bottle and purchase a new one. By the end of the war, thirty-two squadron bottles were in regular use.

Today, the Top of the Mark remains very popular with visitors and the local population. There is a full menu and a live band with dancing. The afternoon offers cocktails and spectacular views of San Francisco and the Pacific Ocean. Enjoy the view and a drink and think about all that has happened in this bar over the past nine decades. Servicemen still frequent the bar. Maybe you will see a couple of our guys having a squadron shot. It's still a tradition.

It was Halloween, and the bartender was asking the crowd if anyone had ever seen a ghost. Well, after much discussion – no, not really seen one. The bartender then asked if anyone had ever spoken to a ghost. No, none had ever really talked to a ghost. Then, the bartender wanted to know if anyone had ever had sex with a ghost. Everyone was laughing and drinking, but then one fellow announced that he had the experience. The bartender asked him to describe having sex with a ghost. The guy said, "Oh, I was sitting over at that table, I thought you said with a goat."

Key West has always been a special place, located 165 miles from Miami and only ninety miles from Cuba. The little city has always attracted a blend of characters, cultures, and customs. There have been Cuban cigar makers, New England ship builders, Bahamian scavengers, and even a few pirates over the years. The tropical climate has enchanted artists, writers, and those wanting to escape everyday life. It was Key West's rowdy atmosphere and exceptional fishing that attracted Ernest Hemingway, and Harry Truman practically moved the White House to Key West beginning in 1946. Hemingway, who would spend a lot of time in France, called Key West the San Trope of the poor.

Two things that forced Key West into the mainstream -- Henry Flagler's railroad from Miami in 1912, and when that was destroyed by a hurricane, the US government extended US Highway 1 all the way from Miami to the island in 1938. Key West has weathered some terrible hurricanes over the years, and the 1930s Great Depression almost destroyed the place. It became home to a lot of freewheeling folks in the 30s. First, Prohibition was in full force, but in Key West, it was regarded as another silly exercise dreamed up by the federal government. One of the most enterprising locals on the scene was Joe Russell, a real Conch, born and raised in Key West. Conch is the term given to Key West natives. It's derived from the tough and tasty mollusks found in the waterways around the keys.

In 1920, Joe Russell was a charter boat captain who had a thirty-two-foot fishing boat named the Anita. Joe Russell became Ernest Hemingway's boat captain, fishing mate, and close friend for the next twelve years. In addition to fishing, the Anita made frequent trips to Havana, returning loaded with liquor. These were tough times, a depression worldwide, and Prohibition offered an opportunity to make some real money. Prohibition ended in 1933, and by then, Joe Russell had saved enough money to open a real, legitimate business, a bar. Typical of Key West, the Blind Pig was a rundown building with no door, sawdust on the floor, pool tables, and open gambling in the rear. You could stay as long as you wanted since the Blind Pig was open twenty-four hours a day, 365 days a year. Beer was a nickel, and drinks were fifteen cents. A year later, a dance floor was added, and it became known as the Silver Slipper. It lasted three and a half years, and the leading customer was Ernest Hemingway and his many buddies and fellow authors. When Hemingway first arrived in Key West, the bank would not cash one of his royalty checks. The bank figured an individual of Hemingway's appearance should not be in possession of a check that big. Hemingway took it over to the Silver Slipper, and Joe Russell cashed it without a question.

Hemingway had been living in Havana and arrived in Key West in April 1928 with his second wife, Pauline Pfeiffer. He was already a well-known author, having published" The Sun Also Rises" in 1926, and he was working on his next novel," A Farewell to Arms."

In 1937, Joe Russell and his landlord got into a dispute over an increase in the rent. Joe had a lease contract that was quite strict, so he waited until the owner left town, and in the middle of the night, Joe and friends moved the entire contents of the Silver

Slipper one block down Duvall Street, where Joe had quietly bought a building at the corner of Duvall and Green street. The bar never actually closed. Customers just picked up their drinks and moved down the street. Joe kept the bar open the rest of the night, and everything was "on the house." When the landlord returned, his building was simply empty. When asked to comment, Hemingway shrugged and said," That's only in Key West." It was Hemingway who chose the name Sloppy Joe's for the new location, named for one of his favorite spots in Havana.

In 1931, Hemingway and his wife Pauline bought a house at 907 Whitehead Street, a short walk from Sloppy Joe's. The Hemingway's spent a lot of money rehabbing the rundown house. They converted the 2nd floor of the carriage house into a studio, and it was here that Hemingway wrote every morning. Some of the author's works written in Key West include 'Islands in the Stream,' 'Old Man and the Sea,' 'Farewell to Arms,' and especially 'To Have and Have Not.' This last novel was about Key West during the depression years. It was Joe Russell who was the book's model for the sea captain, forced to become a smuggler of booze and people or whatever else made money just to avoid poverty. The book was made into a major film in 1944 starring Humphrey Bogart and Lauren Bacall.

Hemingway finished writing around noon each day, and the remainder of the day was spent drinking, carousing, and philosophizing with his friends, known as the Key West mob. This usually wound up late in the evening at Sloppy Joe's.

Hemingway and Pauline lived at 907 Whitehead Street until 1939, raising two sons and installing Key West's first inground swimming pool -- a big one. When Sloppy Joe's underwent rehab in 1930, Hemingway had one of the large urinals removed and placed in his front yard as a fountain. It is still there.

In 1939, Hemingway met his third wife, Martha Gellhorn, at Sloppy Joe's. He and Pauline divorced, and Hemingway moved back to Cuba in December 1939. Pauline remained in the house until her death in 1951. Today, the house is a popular Key West tourist attraction.

Sloppy Joe's is open for business, and it hasn't changed a lot. The place, 80 years later, still has that offbeat ambiance, casual, undemanding, family atmosphere that Joe Russell and his customers loved. The long horseshoe bar is still packed, and the walls are covered with mounted animals and fish, photos, and trophies, many of them from Hemingway. The bar is open until 4am. Every July, there is a Hemingway look-alike contest lasting two days. It is a big celebration attracting over 150 contestants.

Sloppy Joe's remains the famous bar in Key West. But it is definitely not the only interesting saloon this special town offers. When Harry Truman was president, 1945-1953, he had a poker room with a bar staffed by two Navy corpsmen installed at the Winter White House located at the Key West Naval Air Station.

The Hog's Breath Saloon, whose motto is "hogs' breath is better than no breath at all, "was conducting a bartender contest during my visit. Bartenders had gathered from all over the country for the weeklong competition. The idea was for the bartenders to appear individually on an improvised stage where all the ingredients for a special tropical concoction had been assembled. This was a test of skill, quality, and speed. The drink prepared by the contestant, who must be a qualified bartender, was then passed out to the many judges throughout the bar wearing cups around their necks into which the drink was poured. The prize was an ego booster and several thousand dollars. And the same evening at the Schooner Wharf Pub, an entirely different contest was taking place.

The Schooner is an open-air bar with a mostly dirt floor, umbrellas over the tables, and a makeshift roof over the bar—real Key West. An FM radio disc jockey was in charge, and he had selected five male volunteers from the crowd. They were seated at a table facing the audience. The point of the contest was to find which one of the five contestants could down a shot of tequila, one Corona beer, three large tacos, and a chili pepper in the shortest time. This contest was only round one and was immediately followed by five females doing the same thing. Now, this was early in the evening, and the large crowd was having a lot of fun. People were cheering for their favorites, lots of off-color comments from the audience and the announcer, including the size of the Peppers the ladies were swallowing and the girls responding that "size does matter." At the end of the first round, one of the women had a substantial lead.

Down the street at Sloppy Joe's, a vocalist was performing with the band, and another contest was in full swing. Contestants were assembled on the side of the stage, and whenever the vocalist abruptly stopped singing, one of the contestants was selected to finish the song. What made it especially difficult and funny was the vocalist was singing songs no one had ever heard before. Keep in mind all this is accompanied by plenty of drinking and lasts far into the night. This is only a small sample of the nightlife available. If you visit Key West, come prepared to have a good time, and besides, you can go fishing during the day.

The Algonquin hotel was built in 1904 and, although remodeled many times, still stands near the corner of 6th Ave. and W 44th Street in midtown Manhattan. It has about 200 rooms and over the many years it has always been considered "somewhat classy," and definitely expensive. It's well known for a couple of special rooms, the Rose Room, and the Oak Room, and for its special hotel cat.

The original builder intended the Algonquin to be a sort of "Snooty" place catering to the theatrical and literate folks. Its location is on 44th Street, but it is among the Yale, Harvard, and New York Yacht Clubs already located there. It is named for the language spoken by the Native Americans who once lived nearby. Once billed as America's "most comfortable hotel," it has been designated a New York City landmark since 1987.

One of Algonquin's trademarks is the always-present hotel cat. Since the late 1920s, the hotel has always had a lobby cat. It even has a paid "cat officer" to administer to the cat in residence.

The first cat was a feral cat found on Long Island and named Rusty for his marmalade coloring. The actor, John Barrymore, was staying at the hotel at the time and appearing on Broadway as Hamlet in Shakespeare's play. Barrymore decided Rusty wasn't quite the name for an Algonquin cat and renamed him Hamlet. There have been eight Hamlets and three Matildas at the hotel over the past 100 years. One recent Matilda was so "choosey," as cats often tend to be, that she preferred her milk served in a champagne glass. The cat in residence has sleeping quarters provided at the end of the check-in counter and in the front window area, where there is a "do not disturb" sign. The cat makes popular appearances at birthday parties, fashion shows, board meetings, and other hotel functions. It can occasionally be found sleeping out front in one of the planter boxes.

The historical item that has made the Algonquin famous is a group of authors, wits, and theatrical personalities that established a luncheon "get together" that became known as the "Algonquin Round Table."

The original meeting took place in the Oak Room at a long rectangular table. It became known as the "vicious circle." Soon, the manager moved the growing group to a large round table in the Rose Room, and they became the "Algonquin Roundtable" and met every weekday for ten years, from 1919 to 1929. They had lunch and engaged in witty conversation, wisecracks, and discussions of current events. Since several of the members were featured columnists in many New York newspapers and magazines, the proceedings at the luncheons were easily disseminated to the public through the press. Other members were playwrights, authors, and short story contributors. The charter members included Dorothy Parker, critic, and screenwriter; Hayward Braun, columnist, and sportswriter; Robert Benchley, actor; Alexander Wolcott, critic, and journalist; Harold Ross, editor of The New Yorker. Over the ten years, many others attended on an in-and-out basis: Noel Coward, Edna Ferber, Harpo Marx, and Tallulah Bankhead.

A lot has been written about the Round Table, and many of these witty quotes have been published, especially ones contributed by Dorothy Parker.

This is a sampling of a few of the well-known quotes by Dorothy Parker:

"You can lead a horticulture, but you can't make her think."

"I love a martini, two at the most. Three, I'm under the table; four, I'm under the host."

"Ducking for apples. "Change one letter, and you have the story of my life."

"Beauty is only skin deep, but ugliness goes clear to the bone."

"He and I had an office so tiny, any smaller, and it would have been adultery."

After meeting for lunch daily for ten straight years, in 1929, the group broke up. Asked what happened, Frank Case, the manager of the Algonquin, replied, " well, what happened to the 55th Street Reservoir? Nothing lasts forever;" they all went separate ways. Robert Benchley, the actor, and Dorothy Parker, the playwright, both had successful careers in Hollywood. Most of the group stayed in touch and met occasionally over the remaining years.

One more true personal story about the Algonquin hotel. I was employed by a division of the Eastman Kodak company in the advertising department. The Kodak building occupied the block between 43rd and 44th streets on 6th Ave. (Ave. of the Americas). The Algonquin was across the avenue on 44th Street. We went there for lunch or for a drink after work occasionally; the place was not a "hang out" bar. One evening, we were there celebrating something; it seemed we had as many celebrations for things that did not happen as we did for regular birthdays, promotions, etc. On this occasion, one member of our group was leaving to catch his commuter train home. He decided to use the hotel's front door. We all heard this awful sound of shattering glass! Andy had walked through the front door without opening it! There he stood, briefcase in hand, suit, and tie, not a scratch. The whole glass door panel had come loose when he pushed the door, and then it landed on the concrete steps. An old quote must be true: " God has a special Providence for fools, drunkards, and the United States of America," Otto von Bismarck.

The Green Mill is located at 4802 N Broadway Street in Chicago's Uptown neighborhood. It's been there since 1907, first as a bar and beer garden catering to mourners visiting two nearby cemeteries. The owner wanted to name it "The Red Mill" after the Moulin Rouge in Paris, but to avoid association with a nearby "Red Light" district decided to call it the Green Mill. He even installed a green windmill on the roof. The place has been restored, but it still has the stage that's hosted just about every jazz celebrity in the Country over the past 100 years. But it also has the distinction of being the favorite night spot for the mob during Prohibition. Al Capone's favorite booth is still there, situated in the corner where he could keep an eye on both the entrance in the front and the one in the rear. "Machine Gun" McGurn, one of Capone's favorite henchmen, the nickname was earned on the streets of Chicago, owned the bar when it was a Speakeasy in the 1920s.

McGurn is infamous for several incidents: Joe E Lewis, a leading entertainer at the time, had a dispute with McGurn and threatened to take a job at a rival club. So, McGurn slashed his throat; he was a singer and a comedian. This incident is the inspiration for the 1957 movie "The Joker is Wild" starring Frank Sinatra. By the way, Lewis survived the attack.

McGurn is credited with planning the infamous Saint Valentine's Day massacre, which killed seven members of the rival Chicago North Side gang. He also used his Tommy Gun to assassinate the North Side crime boss Hymie Weiss.

Over the years, the Green Mill has been featured in twelve movies. Even today, there is still the access hatch at the end of the bar that leads to a tunnel under Broadway Street to an adjacent building. This is how Capone and others managed to elude authorities when the club experienced a rare raid during Prohibition.

Following the repeal of Prohibition, the Green Mill became a reputable night spot and was Chicago's leading jazz venue. Stars like Al Jolson, Billie Holiday, Texas Guinan, Louis Armstrong, Sophie Tucker, Benny Goodman, and Tommy Dorsey frequently stared as entertainers on the small Green Mill stage.

Today, the Green Mill is considered the oldest continuous-running jazz club in the country. The Green Mill is open seven days a week. There's no cocktail list. Just order what you want, no credit cards, cash only, and no reservations. The nightly entertainment follows the traditional program: opening act, main performance, then a late-night jam session till 4:00 AM closing. There is live music every night and certain nights are special, for example, Thursdays are "big band nights" with plenty of dancing. The inside decor will transport you back 50 years to the heyday of jazz clubs. There is one long, smooth bar that runs down the entire left side, crowned by smokey mirrors and beautiful, old wooden lights. The rear of the room is wood paneling and velvet curtains that serve as the backdrop for the dance floor and slightly elevated main stage. Scattered among the booths and small tables are hundreds of black and white tiles covering the tall wooden support beams. These give the room a touch of old-time glitz and glamour. The nightly crowd consists of a lot of regulars and friends, jazz lovers, and an ample sampling of tourists and first-timers.

The historic Menger Hotel in downtown San Antonio stands on the site of the Battle of the Alamo. The Menger family immigrated from Germany in 1847, settled in San Antonio, and opened a successful brewery. In 1859, the 50-room Menger Hotel opened and became a favorite stop on the famous Chisholm Trail used by cattle drivers moving their cattle to market.

The Menger Hotel and Bar is loaded with history, but one true story stands out. In April 1898, the US and Spain went to war over an incident in Cuba involving an explosion on the USS Maine in the Havana harbor. Colonel Leonard Wood, an Army doctor, was serving as White House physician to President Grover Cleveland at the time. He was also a Congressional Medal of Honor recipient for his medical efforts during the Apache campaign of 1886.

Teddy Roosevelt was serving as Assistant Secretary of the Navy. Wood and Roosevelt decided to raise an "all-volunteer" Calvary regiment to aid the war effort. Fort Sam Houston in San Antonio offered to supply the new regiment with the horses it needed. So, Wood and Roosevelt traveled to Texas and set up a recruiting table at the end of the bar in the Menger Hotel. Teddy

Roosevelt was 39 years old, and Wood made him his assistant with the rank of Lieutenant Colonel. They managed to recruit a total of 1250 Cowboys, Native Americans, merchants, and other assorted adventurers. The most famous volunteer regiment in history was created at the end of the Menger Hotel bar: the "Rough Riders."

The men set up a training camp just outside town in what is now Roosevelt Park. New volunteers continued to join the regiment. When they weren't training, a lot of the Rough Riders spent their time at the Menger bar, where Roosevelt bought the beer. Eventually, Wood made him stop the practice of fraternizing with the enlisted men. The Menger bar still has on display the two tables used by Wood and Roosevelt to recruit the Rough Riders.

Well, the regiment left San Antonio for Tampa, FL. Then, on to Cuba in July 1898, Roosevelt led his regiment up Kettle Hill in San Juan Heights, winning independence for Cuba and fame for Teddy Roosevelt. Colonel Wood rose to Army Chief of Staff while Roosevelt rode his popularity and reputation to become vice president. On September 6, 1901, President McKinley was assassinated, and Roosevelt became America's youngest president at the age of 42. Roosevelt returned to the Menger in 1905 as President to a huge banquet held honoring him and the surviving Rough Riders. There is a major celebration every year in the Menger bar on Roosevelt's birthday, October 27th.

Teddy Roosevelt was eventually awarded the Congressional Medal of Honor for his heroic charge up San Juan Hill. He was the only U.S. President to receive the country's highest military honor. Coincidentally, Teddy Roosevelt, junior, a brigadier general in World War II, was also awarded the Medal of Honor for leading his Fourth Infantry Division ashore in the first wave on Utah beach, D-Day, June 6th, 1944.

One winter evening following a session of parliament, Churchill was having a drink with friends when an aide interrupted to inform him that a "backbench" member of parliament had been caught performing indecent acts with a guardsman in Saint James Park nearby during one of the coldest February nights in over 30 years.

Churchill, a man who had dealt with news such as "the British Army trapped at Dunkirk" or "two of the largest British battleships sunk on the same day at Singapore," sipped his drink, looked up, and said, "makes you proud to be British doesn't it?"

The Pump Room was a bar and restaurant located off the lobby of the Ambassador East hotel at the corner of State Parkway and Gothe Street in Chicago's Gold Coast area on the near north side of town. The Ambassador West was just across the street, connected by a tunnel. Named after an 18th-century spa in Bath, England, the Pump Room opened in October 1938 and reached its heyday in the 1950s and 60s. Every celebrity visiting Chicago could be found at the Pump Room. And if you happened to occupy booth number one, well, you had made it in Chicago. The booth even had its own telephone sitting on the table, really something in the 1950s. The leading Chicago newspaper columnist was Herb Kupcinet with his Kup's gossip column. Kup spent every night either in booth one or hanging around booth one collecting gossip for his column, which appeared the next morning. The original booth is now at the Chicago History Museum.

There have been books written about the Pump Room, movies featuring the Pump Room Alfred Hitchcock's "North by Northwest," and even songs about the Pump Room. It would be difficult to stay at the Ambassador and not encounter some famous personality. My wife and I were on the elevator one evening when the comedian Jackie Mason came aboard. We stepped to the rear of the car on opposite sides. Well, his routine started immediately. "Was it something I had said? Weren't we getting along? Perhaps he could help." It continued until the doors opened on the first floor. That was it. Off he went out the door and into the night.

The manager told us that Jackie Mason arrived about every six months, stayed three or four weeks, left, and returned about six months later. The Ambassador Hotel was placed on the National Register of Historical Sites in 1976.

My introduction to the Pump Room did not begin until the 1970s. We lived in the Chicago suburbs for five years during the 60s but rarely went downtown for dinner. By 1970, I was working as an advertising manager in New York City. Almost every major trade show was held at McCormick Place in Chicago, right on Lake Michigan. As a result, my job took me to Chicago several times a year. We always stayed at the Ambassador East, and we always wound up at the Pump Room either in the early evening after work or later when we returned from dinner.

In 1971, a radio and television sports announcer named Harry Caray arrived in Chicago to begin broadcasting White Sox baseball games after a 25-year career announcing the Saint Louis Cardinal games. His abrupt departure from Saint Louis has always been rumored to have been the result of an affair with the wife of one of Gussie Bushes' sons. Gussie Bush owned Budweiser beer and the Saint Louis Cardinals.

Harry Caray was an instant hit with the White Sox organization and the fans. He was easily recognizable with his oversized, thick, horn-rimmed glasses. He wasn't just a radio announcer; he was a complete entertainer and extremely funny. He had two trademark specialties, shouting "Holy Cow" every time something important happened: a home run, a great catch, etcetera. The other was the 7th inning stretch and his rendition of " Take Me Out to the Ball Game." It wasn't that his voice was good, but it was special, and it was also broadcast on the stadium's public address system. When Harry died at age 83, they played " Take Me Out to the Ball Game" at his funeral in Holy Name Cathedral with every VIP in Major League Baseball and every celebrity from the state of Illinois in attendance.

On my trips to Chicago, I noticed that every time I sat at the Pump Room bar in the early evening, Harry Caray was there drinking and having a wonderful time with a few friends. I learned that Harry and his third wife, Dutchy, lived in a suite at the Ambassador. The hotel had 225 rooms and fifty-five suites. Harry's nightly schedule when he was to broadcast a White Sox home game included having a few drinks at the Pump Room and then heading out to the ballpark for a night's work. But that wasn't the end. In fact, often, it was just the beginning. When the game ended, Harry headed for his late-night spot, Rush Street. This great street was known in the 70s and 80s as "the street of dreams," and Harry was known as the mayor of Rush Street. Rush Street is a one-mile-long, one-way street in Chicago's near north side. In the 70s and 80s, it was lined from one end to the other with bars, nightclubs, and restaurants. It was considered America's biggest entertainment draw outside Las Vegas. Friends often commented the amazing thing about Harry was, "when the hell did he sleep?"

In 1982, Harry moved his announcing skills to Chicago's north side and began his career with the Chicago Cubs for the next 15 years. He was very smart and very successful. In addition to the baseball broadcasting career, he was now on Chicago's WGN radio station, which covered the entire USA. He was also involved in the ownership of seven upscale Chicago restaurants and still drinking and partying all night, every night. It was just a major part of his successful life. During his career, he won every conceivable broadcasting award, including a spot in the Cooperstown Baseball Hall of Fame.

Over his lifetime, Harry Caray had developed a huge base of fans who simply loved him. Harry described himself as a "Cub fan and Bud man." He estimated that over his forty-one years of broadcasting, he averaged 4.9 Budweiser's per day or 1780 per year. This was in addition to the martinis and the Grand Manière's. A few years after his death, a "drinking diary" surfaced that was published in the Chicago Sun-Times newspaper in 1972. Harry spent 288 straight days in bars. He once said, "Either the tales about me are exaggerated, or else I'm simply indestructible."

He was one of those people, Winston Churchill, Ulysses S Grant, and Ernest Hemingway, where alcohol was a big component of their lives. But with Harry, alcohol was just part of the constant partying. He was just having an awfully good time! Harry would be proud of both his son and grandson, two very successful sports announcers.

The Stonewall Inn is a gay bar and national historical site in the Greenwich Village neighborhood of lower Manhattan in New York City. Located at 55 Christopher Street, it was the site of the 1969 riots that are credited with launching the gay rights movement.

In the 1960s, New York State law prohibited serving alcohol to gay patrons. As a result, gay bars were usually registered as private" bottle" clubs that did not require a liquor license. Club patrons had to sign their names in a registry book upon entry in order to preserve the club's false exclusivity. The Genovese crime family controlled most of the gay bars in Greenwich Village. The family bribed the New York 6th police precinct to ignore the activities occurring at the gay clubs.

Without police interference, the mafia could cut a lot of corners; the club lacked fire exits, clean restrooms, or running water behind the bar to clean glasses. Drinks were watered down, and the mafia routinely blackmailed the club's wealthier patrons who wanted to keep their sexual orientation a secret. It was reported that the mafia made far more money from extortion than from the bar. There was a bouncer at the door to *check you out* and make sure you signed the register. Most everyone used a false name.

In spite of all this, the Stonewall became an important gay destination in Greenwich Village. It had a few attractions that other gay bars couldn't offer. It was a big place, and it had two dance floors and a jukebox to provide music. Very few gay bars were able to offer dancing.

Even with the weekly payoffs to the police, known as "Gayola," raids were still a frequent fact of life. Usually, a corrupt cop would tip the management off in time for them to clear the dance floor and hide any other illegal activities that might be occurring.

When the police raided the Stonewall on the hot summer night of June 28th, 1969, in the early morning hours, for some unknown reason, the bar had not been tipped off. Armed with a warrant, the police entered the club, roughed up a couple customers, confiscated bottles of bootleg alcohol, and arrested thirteen people for violating the New York State law prohibiting cross-dressing. Female police officers would take suspects into the bathroom to check their sex.

A fairly large crowd gathered outside the bar and failed to disperse when ordered by the police. At one point, a policeman struck one of the lesbians over the head as he was forcing her into the police van. She shouted to the crowd to step up and do something. For some unknown reason, on this particular night, that is all it took to ignite the crowd. They began to throw whatever they could find at the police: bottles, cobblestones, coins, and shoes. The *Stonewall Riot* had begun. The outnumbered police barricaded themselves in the bar, which the mob outside attempted to set on fire. The fire department and a riot squad were eventually able to put the flames out and disperse the crowd. However, a much larger crowd, thousands, gathered in the area for the next five nights, and the popular Village Voice newspaper kept everyone up to date on the situation.

One year later, on the anniversary, June 28th, 1970, thousands of people marched from the Stonewall Inn to Central Park in what was America's first large gay pride parade. Similar parades took place in Chicago, San Francisco, and Los Angeles.

In 2016, the Stonewall Inn, Christopher Park across the street, and the surrounding area were designated a National Monument in recognition of the area's contribution to gay rights. Today, you can have a drink in a place that is credited with the beginning of the gay rights movement, open seven days a week from 2 pm to 4 am.

A seal went into a bar and pulled up a bar stool. The bartender said what would you like?" seal replied, "Anything but a Canadian Club."

I'm including a favorite bar in Buffalo, NY, because I spent a lot of time there in my early years and because a city like Buffalo has a lot of wonderful bars.

The Anchor Bar, located at 1047 Main Street corner of North Street, was founded in 1935 by Frank and Teresa Bellissimo and opens every day at 11 AM. Officially known as Frank and Therese's Anchor Bar, this is the birthplace of the now world-famous "Buffalo chicken wings." It was closing time on March 4th, 1964, when a large group of bartender Dominic Bellissimo's friends arrived, and they were thirsty and hungry. The kitchen, run by Dominick's mother, Teresa, had already closed. Dominic asked his mother to please put some food together for his buddies. The only thing Teresa could find was a pile of chicken wings, which were usually discarded or sometimes used in the stock pot to prepare soup. Teresa took the chicken wings, deep-fried them, and flavored them with a mixture of butter, cayenne peppers, and a few other spices. She cut up some celery sticks and added blue cheese for dipping as an appetizer. At the time, these were just given away — no charge. Well, the chicken wings were quite a hit around Buffalo, and people began flocking to the Anchor Bar.

Authentic chicken wings are never battered or grilled, only deep-fried and crispy. The sauce is always added after the wings are cooked. The tradition always includes chunky blue cheese and celery sticks.

The Anchor Bar has opened in many other locations, from Toronto, Canada, to three spots in Texas. There is a branch at the Buffalo airport terminal. The original location continues to operate every day of the week. The walls are covered with autographed photos of celebrities who have visited the bar. If you come to Buffalo, you must visit the Anchor Bar, which created the Buffalo Chicken Wing over 60 years ago.

Today, the Anchor Bar serves and ships over 2000 pounds of chicken wings each day. It also ships its special wing sauces in a 12-pack case. Time flew by, and Teresa passed away peacefully where she had lived all her adult life, in her apartment above the bar, in November 1985. She was eighty-four years old. The Buffalo Chicken Wing Festival is held every summer at the downtown baseball stadium and attracts over 40,000 wing lovers. The current chicken wing-eating contest record is 173 wings in twelve minutes! You will need a little bottle of Tums if you try to beat that record!

Pete's Tavern, located at 129 E 18th Street in lower Manhattan, claims to be the oldest continuously operating restaurant/bar in the U.S. since 1864. The location is in the historic and picturesque Gramercy Park area of Manhattan. The building was built in 1829 and was originally the Portman Hotel. It served as a "grocery and grog" store beginning in 1851. In 1899, the place was bought by John and Tom Healy and became "Healey's Cafe." The present name dates to the purchase of the establishment by Peter Belles in 1926.

The original 40-foot rosewood bar, decorated back bar, tin ceiling, and floor have been in place since 1864. The booths and the cabinets above them are also original furniture.

The short story author William Sidney Porter, known by the pen name, O. Henry, lived down the street at 55 Irving Place from 1903-1907 and was a Healey's regular. Healeys appeared in his short story "The Lost Blind" under the name "Keneally's." Local legend claims that O. Henry wrote his well-known story, "The Gift of the Magi," while occupying the second booth from the front in Healey's. This is possible since Porter (O. Henry) wrote 381 short stories during his years in New York, and many of them included observations of New York life and landscape and its residents. Porter wrote a short story for the New York World Sunday magazine every week for over a year.

During Prohibition, 1920 -1933, the place became a florist shop. The location, close to Tammany Hall, the political machine that ran New York City during the 1920s and the 30s, was only three blocks away. These politicians needed a bar to conduct their business and celebrate their deals. Signs outside, along with boxes of flowers, invited passers-by to come in and purchase roses, violets, and gardenias. A side door led to a dining room, and with the proper password, you could open a dummy refrigerator door and enter the bar.

Due to its appearance, both outside and indoors, Pete's has appeared in many films and TV programs. These include Two for the Season, Seinfeld, Ragtime, Law and Order, Sex in the City, Fleishman is in Trouble, and numerous others. Pete's has also been used for TV commercials and print advertising, Miller Lite beer, and many others.

During the summer months, Pete's has one of the oldest operating outdoor cafes in New York. This is especially charming because of its location in the Gramercy Park Historical District.

Inside, the walls are covered with photos depicting the history of New York City, from horse-drawn wagons to speeding yellow cabs, Pete's Florist shop, and lots of celebrity photos. Upstairs, the dining rooms have their original hardwood floors and exposed brick walls, 200 years old.

Located at the corner of 18th Street and Irving Place, Pete's is open from noon to 2 AM daily.

A little cowboy went up to heaven, and Saint Peter met him at the pearly gates. Welcome, Fred. We are glad to see you. Before you go into heaven, the Lord has asked me to conduct a special survey of newcomers for the next few weeks. You were down there on earth for quite a while, Fred. Do you have something you're really proud of that we could record in the "good deeds book?"

Fred replied immediately, "Yes, I do. I was coming out of Joe's saloon, my favorite place, and got on my horse. I noticed a bunch of biker boys harassing a group of young ladies over in the corner of the parking lot. So, I rode over, got off my horse, and walked up to the biggest, meanest looking one, the leader, and told them to get on their motorcycles and disperse, or I would beat the crap out of the whole bunch! Nobody even moved, so I slapped that leader right across the face just as hard as I could."

"Wow," says Saint Peter," Fred, that is exactly the type of story the Lord wants to hear. When did this all happen?" Fred replies, "Actually, it was just a couple of minutes ago."

Billy Bob's, 2520 Rodeo Plaza, Fort Worth, Texas, is billed as the biggest "honky tonk" bar in the world, and it is really big. It is the total opposite of a cozy Irish pub. The original building dates to 1910 as an open-air cattle barn at the Fort Worth Stockyards. In 1936, the city enclosed the structure, and it became the site for cattle auctions. During World War II, the building became an airplane factory. After the war, it was converted to a department store so large the salesclerks wore roller skates to move around.

On April 1, 1981, April Fool's Day, Billy Bob's opened with a lot of publicity. It had 100,000 square feet of entertainment space with over 30 bar stations, a full professional bull riding ring, and a wonderful Texas-sized dance floor. It was open every day and night and had a capacity of 6000 people. That is when it assumed the title of the world's largest "honky tonk."

Billy Bob's has been going strong for over forty-two years, with crowds dancing, drinking, attending live rodeos, and enjoying a never-ending line of famous entertainers. Billy Bob's has been named "Country Music Club of the Year" twelve times by the Academy of Country Music. There's a large photo display of past entertainers with autographed mementos of their visits; everyone in country music has entertained at Billy Bob's.

Merle Haggard was a big country music star in the 70s and 80s. He was appearing with George Jones on stage at Billy Bob's on March 21st, 1983. They were introducing a duet on a new album, and one of the hit songs was "CC Water back," which is bar talk for a Canadian Club with a water chaser. Well, Merrill got carried away with the enthusiastic reception they were receiving and decided to buy a Canadian Club whiskey "for the house." That particular purchase holds the Guinness Book of Records title for the biggest round of drinks ever bought, 5095 shots of Canadian Club whiskey, over forty gallons. When owner Billy Bob Barnett brought the bill over to Haggard, he offered to buy him a drink, and Merrill accepted the offer. The total bill was $12,757.50. At today's prices, the bill would be over $40,000.

Many episodes of the popular TV show "Dallas" were filmed at Billy Bob's. Over a dozen movies have used the place to film bar scenes: *Over the Top, Sylvester Stallone,* 1987. *Baja Oklahoma, Willie Nelson,* 1988. *Pure Country, George Strait,* 1992.

And the stage is not limited to country music. Everyone from Bob Hope and Ray Charles to Ringo Starr has entertained at Billy Bob's. Professional bull riding takes place every Friday and Saturday night. What could be more fun than going to a bull riding contest in a bar? There is a house band for dancing and entertainment every night. In fact, in his early years, George Strait was the" house band" at Billy Bob's.

On a personal basis, in 1981, we had a business sales meeting in Fort Worth, and in the evening, about 20 of us went to Billy Bob's and had a great time. I remember the entire group, all men, on the dance floor taking line dancing lessons with a couple of gorgeous cowgirl instructors. Billy Bob's has, fittingly, a big menu from the "honky tonk kitchen," serving everything from catfish and prime steaks to jalapeno burgers and footlong corn dogs.

This is a place where you are going to have a good time. It has everything, a bull ring, a dance floor, music, live entertainment, and over thirty separate bars. You are just bound to find a spot that fits your wants.

The King Cole Bar is located in the historic, stately Saint Regis hotel at 2 E 55th Street In Manhattan. The Saint Regis is a posh hotel built by John Jacob Astor the 4th and opened in 1904. It has been a major attraction for the rich and famous since day one. The name comes from the upper Saint Regis Lake in the Adirondack mountains. When it opened, the hotel was located in a neighborhood of numerous wealthy private homes, including homes for the Rockefellers and the JP Morgan's. In its early years, the hotel was mainly a residence for the upper echelon of wealthy New Yorkers. Salvador Dali lived at the hotel for over ten years. John Lennon and Yoko Ono lived there before moving to the Dakota building. Several movies have been filmed at Saint Regis, including *Devil Wears Prada* and *First Wives Club*.

The King Cole is located on the first floor of the Saint Regis. The bar is usually given credit as the birthplace of the "Bloody Mary," originally called the "Red Snapper." Introduced by bartender Ferdinand Patio in 1934.

The main attraction of the King Cole bar is the eight-foot by 30 feet mural covering the entire wall behind the bar. The painting was commissioned by John Jacob Astor for an earlier hotel, the Knickerbocker, on the corner of Broadway and 42nd Street. The artist, Mayfield Parish, was a Quaker and reluctant to paint a mural for a bar, but Astor's offer of $5000, a lot of money in 1906, changed his mind. Astor chose the nursery rhyme "Old King Cole" as the theme for the painting and felt for the money he was spending, he should be portrayed as the king. The painting was moved to the Saint Regis in the mid-1930s and launched Parish's art career. It is currently valued by Sotheby's auction house at 12 million dollars.

Legendary tales of the painting hold that Parish's friends challenged him to paint King Cole in the act of producing flatulence (farting). If you look closely at the King, you will notice his rear is elevated slightly off the seat. In addition, the king has a somewhat sheepish grin, and the knights on either side appear to be startled, and their fingers are at their noses. It's a great story and will keep you occupied as you sip those Bloody Mary's, which currently cost twenty-five dollars each!

Another well-known mural graces the wall behind the bar in the Yankee Doodle tap room at the Nassau Inn in Princeton, NJ. The Nassau Inn is a wonderful small hotel located at Palmer Square in the heart of downtown Princeton, just steps from the university. The mural painted by Norman Rockwell in 1937 on canvas attached to the masonry wall took over nine months to complete. The thirteen-foot-wide piece includes 19 people, two dogs, one pony, and one goose. Of course, Yankee Doodle is riding to town on his pony with a feather in his cap. The special thing about the painting is the typical Rockwell attention to detail, so all nineteen people have separate and very special expressions on their faces. The painting has grown very valuable along with all of Norman Rockwell's works. It is owned by the university and insured for several million dollars.

The bar room also includes a photo wall of famous Princeton graduates, and there are many of them, including actors Jimmy Stewart and Brooke Shields, as well as business leaders Meg Whitman and Jeff Bezos.

The nearly 100-year-old oak tables in the tap room display the carvings of students, faculty, and friends over the years and include some famous names, including Albert Einstein, who lived nearby at 112 Mercer Street from 1933 until his death in 1955. Einstein was a frequent lecturer at Princeton and was associated with the nearby Institute for Advanced Study.

Bemelmans's Bar is located in the Carlyle Hotel at 35 E 76th Street on Manhattan's swank Upper East Side. This place is classy. All the superlatives apply: sophisticated, upscale, glamorous, and, as you might expect, very expensive. And so is the hotel.

Bemelmans's Bar has a legendary piano, and the place opened in 1947 and has been at the top of the New York social scene ever since.

The general manager of the hotel was a close friend of Ludwig Bemelmans. Bemelmans was a German-born successful illustrator for most of the New York magazines: Vogue, New Yorker, Town, and Country. He had become well known for a series of illustrated children's books titled "Madeline." Madeline was a fictional French girl who attended school with eleven other girls in Paris. Her trademarks included a blue coat and a big white hat, and her adventures were the book's subjects.

The manager of the Carlyle commissioned Bemelmans to paint large murals to cover the four walls of the Carlyle's new bar. Bemelmans chose to paint whimsical scenes of New York's Central Park, depicting the park in winter, spring, summer, and autumn. The scenes include both people and animals. A dressed-up rabbit is smoking a cigar, a flock of sheep "mowing" the park grass, an elephant with a parasol and wearing ice skates, a group of squirrels having a picnic, and a gentleman handing a bouquet of balloons to a little girl. These murals are praiseworthy and interesting and became an immediate major New York attraction. They still rank as a big attraction. It took Bemelmans a couple of years to complete the murals; for payment, he accepted eighteen months of free lodging for himself and his family at the hotel. For the price of rooms at the Carlyle, this was a good deal for Ludwig.

The other attraction at the bar is music seven days a week, 365 days a year. Over the past 75 years, most of history's great jazz pianists have appeared at the Carlyle bar. Piano music begins each day at 5:30 PM, and the jazz duo or trio comes on around 8:00 PM. There is a sizeable cover charge per person at both the bar and the tables.

The bar setting is very nice; chocolate brown banquets, a grand piano in the corner, a black granite bar, nickel-edged glass tables with candles, a 24-karat gold leaf ceiling, and, of course, the murals covering the walls. In the afternoon, the wealthy Upper East Side mothers stop by for a drink and a "Shirley Temple" to show the children the murals. At 5:30, folks begin stopping in for a cocktail, and around 8:00 PM, the jazz takes over.

The Carlyle Hotel and Bemelmans's Bar have always attracted celebrities. Jack and Jackie Kennedy stayed here frequently both before and after he was elected president. Jackie lived at the Carlyle for a while following the assassination of the President. The British royal family, including Princess Diana, have always used the Carlyle. On occasion, stars have joined the entertainment in the bar, including Eartha Kitt, Bono, and Liza Minelli. The staff boasts that they know over half the guests. This place is expensive, but it is a marvelous experience.

Musso's and Frank's opened on September 27th, 1919, and it has been Hollywood's number-one spot ever since. Located at 6667 Hollywood Blvd., it was originally owned by Frank Toulet and Joseph Musso. In 1927, the pair sold the restaurant to two Italian immigrants, John Mosso, and Joseph Carissimi. Today, the restaurant is owned and operated by John Mosso's three granddaughters and their children.

The key attraction for Musso's is the "exclusive backroom," guarded by a serious maître-'d; the backroom became a legendary private space reserved for the Hollywood elite. Today, the restaurant has a new room. The light fixtures, the furnishings, and the famous mahogany bar are the originals from 1934.

This special place is still open daily. When you sit down in one of those worn leather booths, peruse a menu that is over 100 years old, or move up to the mahogany bar, you are enjoying Hollywood history and wonderful food. The payphone was the first one installed in Hollywood. How many deals were discussed on that phone, and how many contracts were signed and toasted with one of Musso's famous martinis. Remember, "nothing ever happens over a salad." These people were at Musso's on a daily basis for lunch, dinner, or just drinks. Charlie Chaplin was a regular from the beginning, lunching with Mary Pickford, Rudolph Valentino, and Douglas Fairbanks. Legend has it that Chaplin would frequently challenge Fairbanks to a horse race down Hollywood Blvd. the winner picked up the lunch check. Musso's was open all day, and Greta Garbo and Gary Cooper were frequent breakfast companions in the backroom in the 20s and 30s. In the 50s, the crowd switched to Marilyn Monroe and Joe DiMaggio enjoying drinks. Other regular stars at Musso's included Rita Hayworth, Jimmy Stewart, and Groucho Marx.

When the movie studio executives began to recruit America's best authors to Hollywood, Musso's added another group to the backroom crowd. The Screen Writers Guild happened to be located right across the street, and Stanley Rose's bookshop was the neighbor on the east side of Musso's. America's great writers could be found actually working into the night by the light of the back room's four great chandeliers. F. Scott Fitzgerald, William Faulkner, and Raymond Chandler used Musso's as a second home. Faulkner met his mistress at Musso's, and the relationship lasted twenty years and he was so friendly with the staff he would go behind the bar and make his own drinks. Chandler wrote the final chapters of the *Big Sleep* while sipping drinks in one of the booths in the backroom. As the years went by, the literary crowd continued to be attracted to Musso's. TS Elliot, William Saroyan, Aldous Huxley, John Steinbeck, and Dorothy Parker were all frequent guests.

Lease problems closed the backroom in 1955, and the bar moved to what was christened the *new room*. The literary tradition with a new generation of writers continued. Now, we had Kurt Vonnegut and Joseph Heller occupying the famous bar. Isn't it wonderful that you can make a reservation today, go into this 100-year-old bar/ restaurant, and have a drink and dinner? The menu has barely changed-- but the prices sure have-- and think about all the wonderful people who were regulars at Musso's.

A little cowboy left the bar, went outside, and found someone had painted his horse green. The little guy stomped back into the crowded bar, hopped up on a barstool, and shouted, "Who is the wise bastard that painted my horse green?" The biggest, meanest-looking cowboy at the end of the bar stood up and said, "I did. You having a problem with that?" The little guy paused for an instant and shouted back, "No, but I think he needs a second coat."

The period in American history known as the "Wild West" only lasted for about fifty years, from 1850 to 1900. The movie industry will make sure it endures forever with its films of cowboys, Indians, cattle rustlers, and pioneers, along with occasional hangings, gun fights, and saloons. Prescott, Arizona, was the typical frontier town in the Wild West days. Prescott is in the center of Arizona, about 100 miles north of Phoenix. Today, it's mainly a tourist and retirement town with a growing population of around 46,000.

Beginning in the 1860s, Prescott has a rich history as a frontier gold and silver mining town. Native American Indian tribes also lived in the area, including Apache and the Yavapai, and this resulted in frequent conflict. Fort Whipple was established nearby and served as a home base for soldiers campaigning against the natives.

The Main Street of Prescott was constructed entirely of wood and burned to the ground on three separate occasions. In the early 1900s, it was rebuilt entirely of brick and masonry. The Palace bar and restaurant at 120 S Montezuma Street in the heart of "whiskey row" is Arizona's oldest saloon. It is situated on Whiskey Row, which in Prescott's Boomtown heyday had forty bars, door to door, the length of the street. It's a little hard to imagine 40 bars on one street in the heart of any town or city. What were these people thinking?

The building was erected in 1877 and named the Palace Saloon. This place has quite a history, much of it violent. Famous frontier cowboys Doc Holiday, Wyatt Earp, and his brother Virgil all spent time at the Palace before heading South to Tombstone for their famous shootout with the Clantons at the OK Corral. Wyatt Earp was involved in numerous gunfights and killed two men in the alley behind the saloon. Doc Holiday killed a man in a knife fight inside the Palace.

When the Palace reopened in 1884, after a fire, it had a brand new Brunswick bar. These were the days when these frontier towns took great pride in their bar and pool table if they had one. Other towns might be proud of their church, park, or museum, but for Western places, the bar was the" big deal." The bar in the Palace had been shipped around South America and the Cape of Good Hope to California. It was brought overland by a mule pack train. This was a hand-carved Brunswick bar, the very best!

During the fire of 1900, which pretty much destroyed Whiskey Row, patrons actually carried the beloved Brunswick bar out onto the street and saved it from the blaze.

The upstairs of the Palace was once a very active brothel, which resulted in many problems. Poker tables in the rear contributed to the violence. Doc Holiday's common-law wife, known by the awful nickname of "Big Nose Kate," was a prostitute at the Palace. The basement of this saloon served various purposes: it was a jail, an opium den, and during Prohibition, 1920-1932, it was, of course, a speakeasy.

In 1996, the Palace, once again, underwent a major renovation. This time, the owners restored the interior to its grand original style: swinging front doors, hardwood floors, oak wainscoting, and leaded glass windows.

Today, most of the forty saloons on Whiskey Row have been transformed into small shops, boutiques, and other tourist attractions. The buildings are still there, and the Palace Saloon, with all its western frontier and wild west history, is open seven days a week, serving steak, potatoes, and drinks at the hand-carved Brunswick Bar.

The Carousel Bar is located off the lobby of the Hotel Monteleone at 214 Royal Street in the famous French Quarter of New Orleans. The Monteleone was originally built in 1886 and remodeled many times. Named for its original owner, Antonio Monteleone, it currently has 570 rooms and 50 suites. It has a history of being a favorite destination for Southern writers. The list is long and includes Tennessee Williams, William Faulkner, Ernest Hemingway, and Truman Capote. Capote always claimed he was born there. His mother did stay at the Monteleone during her pregnancy, but records show she made it to the local hospital for the birth. The hotel has been designated a History Landmark by the American Library Association, a distinction held by only two other American hotels, the Plaza and the Algonquin, in New York City.

The Carousel Bar is usually number one, or close to it, in any ranking of favorite and famous American bars. The bar was installed in 1949. The 25-seat circular bar overlooks Royal Street and the adjacent lounge with booths and tables and featuring live entertainment. The bar turns on 2000 large rollers powered by a 1/4 horsepower motor. It makes one complete revolution every fifteen minutes. The bar is often praised as beautiful, and it's designed to be a replica of the famous amusement park merry-go-rounds of the 19th and early 20th centuries. The bar was renovated in 1992, and fiber optics were installed in the ceiling to create the appearance of stars in the night sky. One shooting star crosses the sky at regular intervals for a little excitement.

Both the bar and the lounge are usually crowded in the evenings, and the atmosphere promotes a good time with plenty of conversation and laughter. My wife and I spent several evenings at the Carousel Bar, and it was a great experience every time. In its early days, the adjacent room was a famous nightclub, the Swan Room, where celebrities like Liberace, Louis Prima, and Louis Armstrong appeared. The lounge still features name entertainment and plenty of New Orleans jazz. And don't forget to sample those famous special New Orleans cocktails: the Sazerac, the Hurricane, Ramos gin fizz, and Brandy milk punch. Sazerac is New Orleans' most famous alcoholic drink and dates from the 1830s. Ingredients include absinthe, simple syrup, Peychaud bitters, and rye whiskey. Rye whiskey has replaced the original use of cognac.

The Vieux Carre is the Carousel's s most famous cocktail. Created in 1930 by Hotel Monteleone's head bartender, Walter Bergeron, it consists of cognac, Benedictine, rye whiskey, sweet vermouth, angostura bitters, and Peychaud bitters. It's not something you want to fix at home unless you have a well-stocked bar!

The Old Talbot Tavern was built in 1779 and has never closed since it opened. Located on the town square in historic Bardstown, Kentucky, across from the courthouse and next to the county jail. It's the oldest bourbon bar in America and probably the oldest structure in the state of Kentucky.

The original Tavern had stone walls two feet thick, heavy ceiling timbers, and two fireplaces for cooking food. Interestingly, it had two guest rooms on the second floor, one for men and one for women. In the early colonial days, everyone slept in one room, often in the same bed. Separate guest rooms did not arrive in the United States until the 19th century. The Tavern was the westernmost Stagecoach stop on the line that ran back to Virginia and Philadelphia. Daniel Boone was a frequent visitor, and future presidents Andrew Jackson, William Henry Harrison, and Abraham Lincoln all stayed at the Tavern. Lincoln stayed there with his parents when they were involved in a land dispute that they eventually lost, and they moved on to Indiana. A few other famous guests included Henry Clay, James Audubon, and Jesse James, who got drunk one night and shot the birds painted on the wall by Audubon.

Today, almost 250 years after it first opened, the Old Talbot still offers five bed-and-breakfast guest rooms, each named for a former guest who now haunts the place. The bar offers a generous selection of Kentucky bourbons, and the place opens every day at 11 am for lunch and dinner. It was placed on the National Register of Historic Places in 1973.

You can have a nice dinner, a few bourbons, and stay in a room haunted by the ghost of Jesse James.

Bardstown claims to be the" bourbon capital of the world," with eleven distilleries located within sixteen miles of the town square: Makers Mark, Jim Beam, and Heaven Hill are just a few of the famous ones.

Round Robin Bar, Willard Hotel, Washington, DC

President John Kennedy Booth, Union Oyster House, Boston

Last Chance Saloon, Oakland, CA

Jack London, Author

Tootsies, Nashville, TN

My Brothers Denver, CO

Mc Sorely's Pub, New York City

Mc Sorely's Pub, New York City

Warren Tavern, Charlestown, MA

Warren Tavern

Fraunces Tavern, New York City

The Long Room, Fraunces Tavern, New York City

City Tavern, Philadelphia, PA

Christiana Campbells - Williamsburg

Wayside Tavern, Sudbury, MA

Henry Wadsworth Longfellow

Stork Club, New York City

Sherman Billingsley, Owner

Lady Nancy Astor

Winston Churchill

Eagle Pub, Cambridge, England

Ceiling RAF Bar, Eagle Pub

Grenadier Pub, London, England

Grenadier Pub, London, England Money Stuck to Ceiling

Connaught Hotel Bar, London, England

Prospect-of-Whitby Pub, London, England

Olde Cheshire Cheese Pub, London, England

The Globe Pub, Dunfrie, Scotland

The Round Robin Bar is in the Willard International Hotel at 1401 Pennsylvania Ave. NW in downtown Washington, DC, about two blocks from the White House. Some type of lodging facility has occupied this corner since 1810, over 200 years ago. The Round Robin Bar dates from 1847, and the current hotel was built in 1901.

In the 1800s, Nathaniel Hawthorne called the Willard Hotel and Round Robin Bar "the center of Washington," not the Capitol building or the White House. Every U.S. President and vice president has either stayed at the Willard Hotel or attended a function at the hotel. Assassination threats on Abraham Lincoln were so numerous he was secretly lodged at the Willard from February 20th until his inauguration on March 4th, 1861. A peace Congress with delegates from the Northern and Southern states was convened at the Willard in February 1861 in an attempt to avoid the Civil War. The Willard is listed in the National Registry of Historical Places.

After viewing from her room window Union soldiers marching down Pennsylvania Ave. and off to war, Julia Ward House wrote the words to the *Battle Hymn of the Republic*. One hundred years later, in August 1963, in his room at the Willard, Martin Luther King wrote the finishing paragraph of his, *I Have a Dream* speech. Ironic!

With all this history associated with the hotel, you can imagine the stories belonging to the Round Robin Bar. Jimmy Hughes has tended bar at the Round Robin for over 30 years. He also has a background and education in history. Hughes gives frequent talks and offers history programs about the bar and about Washington. He even has an authentic, handwritten recipe for the mint julep written by Henry Clay. Henry Clay served in the House and Senate as the delegate from Kentucky for 40 years. He is credited with bringing a barrel of Kentucky bourbon and introducing the mint julep at the Round Robin, where it remains the signature drink of the bar.

A bartender at the Round Robin for over thirty years, Hughes has served drinks to many US Presidents, never while in office and only before or after serving as president. His favorite was Gerald Ford, who he described as "down to earth" and very funny. Ford drank Scotch or Budweiser beer. Everyone gives Ford credit for giving up drinking to support his wife, who had a well-publicized drinking problem.

Round Robin's customer base over the years has included famous people other than politicians. The early years included regulars Mark Twain and Walt Whitman, British, and other European royalty, and an endless list of American business leaders who continued to stop by the Round Robin on their visits to Washington. There will always be deals to make, business to be handled, and occasions to be celebrated. Right now, you can visit this 200-year-old, gorgeous mahogany, circular, twelve-seat bar with red leather cushions and famous people's portraits on the wall and perhaps feel a part of American history for a little while. One or two of Jim Hughes's signature mint juleps might help set the mood.

The Union Oyster House is the oldest restaurant in Boston and possibly the oldest restaurant in continuous operation in the U.S. The building has stood on Union Street as a major landmark for over 250 years. Before it became a bar and seafood house, the building housed a fancy dress shop and dry goods business. At this time, the Boston waterfront was at the back door of the shop, making it easy to deliver goods shipped from Europe.

The printer, Isaiah Thomas, published a newspaper on the second floor. "The Massachusetts Spy" is considered the oldest newspaper in the United States. The first stirrings of the coming

American Revolution began to appear in the paper around 1771. By 1775, the Capens Silk and Dry Goods store had become the headquarters for the paymaster of the Continental Army. During the war, the wives of Hancock, Adams, and others met at Capen's to sew clothes for the Army.

By 1796, the future king of France lived on the 2nd floor. At the time, he was exiled from France and supported himself by teaching French to many of Boston's wealthy young ladies. Louis Philippe returned to France and served as king from 1830 -1848.

Capen's Dry Goods closed in 1826, and Atwood and Bacon's restaurant opened. The early part of the 19th century featured an "oyster craze" in America. There were oyster parlors, oyster cellars, oyster saloons, and oyster houses in every town. The new owners installed what became the fabled semi-circular oyster bar at Atwood and Bacon's. It was at this oyster bar where Daniel Webster, a frequent customer, drank his daily tumbler of brandy and water with each half-dozen oysters, usually having at least six plates.

Since 1826, the Oyster House has had only three owners. The Milano family has owned the place since 1970.

The Kennedy family has frequented the Oyster House for years. President John Kennedy preferred the privacy of the upstairs dining room. His favorite booth, #18, "the Kennedy booth," has been dedicated in his honor.

The building was listed as a National Historic Landmark on May 27th, 2003. Located at 41 Union Street, one block from historic Faneuil Hall on the Freedom Trail. Open daily from 11 to 10 PM. There is a regular old-fashioned saloon bar in addition to the famous oyster bar.

Two strangers were sitting at the bar. One turned to the other and said, "Say, do you happen to know the difference between a man's penis and a chicken leg?" The other fellow replied," No, I don't believe I do." The first fellow says, "How would you like to go on a picnic?"

If Bemelmans's Bar on New York's Upper East Side is at the top of the list for class and sophistication, Heinold's Last Chance Saloon near the Wharf in Oakland, CA, is certainly near the bottom. This place was originally constructed in 1880 from wood salvaged from a whaling vessel. For the first three years, it served as a bunkhouse for workers in the nearby oyster beds. In 1883, John Heinold purchased the building and converted it into a pub he named JM Heinold's Saloon. The reason I have included it is due to its very close relationship with the American author Jack London during his early years in Oakland. Not only did London drink here, but he also wrote here and obtained much of the material for his many books here.

To explain the significance of the Last Chance Saloon, I will spend a few paragraphs describing Jack London.

London was an Oakland native born in 1876. He became an important novelist, journalist, and activist. He was one of the very first American authors to become an international celebrity. London was also an adventurer, spending a year in the far north and another year attempting to sail around the world in a boat he built and called the "Snack." As a writer, he attempted to write 1000 words every single day.

The book that made Jack London instantly famous at twenty-seven years old was *The Call of the Wild*, published in 1903. The book sold out immediately and has never been "out of print" since. Published in 47 languages and featured in three major movies and several TV shows. The first movie was silent in 1923; the 2nd in 1935 featured Clark Gable and Loretta Young; in 1972, the star was Charlton Heston. The book is rather short, 232 pages, about a dog named Buck who is leading a civilized and comfortable life in Southern California when he is stolen and sold to traders. The traders take Buck to the Yukon, where there is a heavy demand for sled dogs in the *gold rush*. Buck is transformed into a primitive animal fighting every day to survive. He eventually becomes a strong leader of a pack of dogs in the wild.

This book remains popular and is read in schools around the Country today. London was a prodigious writer and had several best sellers, including "White Fang," "The Seawolf" and "Martin Eden." London was an awesome worker. He published 50 novels between 1900 and 1916, plus hundreds of short stories and journal articles. London passed away at the young age of 40 from gastrointestinal poisoning and a lifetime of hard work.

Heinold's saloon became very popular due to its central location near the ferry from Oakland to Alameda, which was a dry county. Heinold's was "last chance" for a drink before boarding the ferry. It was also located near the wharves where the fishing fleet docked. So Heinold's was the "last chance" for a drink for fishermen leaving for a long voyage at sea. Many a sailor wrote his name on a bill and pinned it to the ceiling, hoping it would still be there when he returned to buy himself a drink. The popular nickname stuck, and pretty soon Heinold's was known as the "Last Chance Saloon."

Jack London claimed he began hanging out at the "Last Chance" when he was 10 years old. When he was 17 and had returned to high school, he used to study at one of the corner tables in the bar. John Heinold always liked him and eventually told London he would pay his tuition to attend the nearby University of California. London attended the University for only one year. He then went to the Yukon for the gold rush and returned to the sea life, and spent a year as a hobo. In between these adventures, he spent his time at the "Last Chance Saloon." It was here that he met the seafaring and waterfront characters that play such a major part in his many adventure novels.

London met and became a close friend of Captain Alexander McLean, head of a seal-hunting fleet. In London's autobiographical "John Barleycorn," the Last Chance is mentioned seventeen times.

The bar has not changed a lot since Jack London sat at one of the tables that are still there and wrote one of his stories. The walls and ceiling are covered with business cards and hats, and even some of the sailor's money is still there. There is a pair of boxing gloves belonging to the champion Bob Fitzsimmons and another pair of Jim Jeffries' gloves. John Heinold's hat is here, along with the original mahogany bar that is still in use. All this isn't fancy or pretty, but this saloon, in this building with this same bar and much of the furniture, has been serving customers for 150 years and counting.

The original gas lighting still illuminates the place, one of the few spots left in California. The original potbellied stove was used as the only source of heat until 1982; it still stands in the middle of the floor. There are a lot of mementos behind the bar and a wonderful wall of photos featuring old pictures of the place. Johnny Heinold's son, George, was quite a hero in France during the First World War, and there is a special display of his many medals on the wall. This is ironic since John was a German immigrant. One of the most unique characteristics of the place is the floor, which is slanted from the front to the rear. This is a result of the famous San Francisco earthquake of 1906. The quake caused some of the pilings supporting the saloon to sink deeper into the ground. There is an old clock in the corner where the hands stopped at 5:18 am, the exact moment of the earthquake.

The current owners are dedicated to making every effort to keep the place as close to the original as possible. Located at Jack London Square and is open every day from 12 noon to 9pm.

Tootsie's Orchid Lounge is a *honky tonk* legend in Nashville, TN. The legend began in 1960 when Hattie Louise "Tootsie" Bess bought a bar named Moms. One day, she came to work to find a painter she hired had decided to paint the entire building orchid purple. From that day on, Moms became known as the "Orchid Lounge." Tootsie's is located behind the Ryman Auditorium, which was home to the Grand Ole Opry from 1943 to 1974. Tootsie's location was perfect to attract up-and-coming stars that appeared on the Opry show. A few of the names include Roger Miller, Patsy Cline, Willie Nelson, Loretta Lynn, and Waylon Jennings. Tootsie collected photos of these artists as they became famous and put them on the wall, which has become known as Tootsies' Wall of Fame. During the early years, Tootsie's bar became quite popular. Noted especially for her kindness, the artists loved her because she took care of them. For the young struggling songwriters and musicians, Tootsie was a small finance company, a booking agent, and especially a counselor. Tootsie established herself and the bar as a valuable part of the Nashville music scene.

In 1974, the Grand Ole Opry moved to a brand-new Opryland entertainment complex, and the Orchid Lounge fell on very hard times. In addition, Tootsie passed away in 1978.

The whole area deteriorated, and by 1990, Tootsies was in danger of closing. Along came Steve Smith, who would not let it close. He purchased the place, and with dedication and hard work, by 2000, the Orchid was thriving once again. The entire surrounding area experienced a revival. Even the Ryman Auditorium was remodeled and began hosting some Opry shows.

Today, the Orchid Lounge hosts bands playing on all three floors, and the place is packed every night of the week. Tootsie's is known as "Honkey Tonk boot camp," and it continues its tradition of helping showcase young up-and-coming stars. Several movies have been filmed at Tootsie's, including *Coal Miner's Daughter* starring Sissy Spacek. The Country Music Hall of Fame Museum has honored Tootsies with a photo exhibit showing key moments in Tootsie's long association with the country music scene. Located at 422 Broadway, Nashville, and is open every day beginning at 11 AM. The food is good, and they still serve Loretta Lynn's favorite Tootsie lobster tail plate. There is a special drink called Tootsie's Apple Pie Moonshine, served in a jar with a screw top, also available online.

The oldest bar in Denver has a fascinating history. My Brother's Bar can be difficult to find since it has no sign out front. The original bar dates from 1873. When the current owners bought it over forty years ago, they didn't have enough money for a sign. The owners were two brothers from Detroit, and they developed a scheme used when vendors had questions about payment. They would say, "I don't know. It's my brother's place." Eventually, someone decided it would be a proper name for the bar. Well, at that time, they had plenty of money for a sign, but they felt they didn't need one, so forty years later, there was no sign for the oldest bar in town.

My Brother's Bar has some unusual characteristics in addition to having no sign. There is also no TV, has never been any TV, and classical music is always in the background. Another quirk is that Girl Scout cookies have always been available for free from behind the bar.

The bar was a favorite hangout for Neil Cassidy and his friend Jack Kerouac during Kerouac's "On the Road" days. Kerouac became a celebrity and an icon for the "Beat Generation" of the 1960s. Cassidy was the central character in the book, which dealt in a very outspoken way with drugs and sex while traveling the USA and Mexico with Cassidy. It was so graphic that most publishers rejected it as too obscene. It took Kerouac quite a while to locate someone who would accept the risk, but Viking Press finally came through.

While serving time at the Colorado State Prison, Cassidy wrote a letter to a friend saying he and Kerouac had been frequent patrons at My Brothers Bar. He felt he owed them a small amount of money to settle the tab. If you happen to be in the vicinity, drop in and give them three or four dollars for me. We don't know if the friend ever honored the request.

Kerouac went on to publish 12 more novels and even greater fame in the hippie and drug culture of the Beat Generation. He lived in Saint Petersburg, Florida, and passed away at age forty-seven from an abdominal hemorrhage caused by a lifetime of excessive drinking.

A couple of years ago, the brothers, in their 80s, were ready to retire. A developer offered them three million dollars for the property, which they planned to raze and construct retail space. Thankfully, this wonderful little bit of Denver's past was preserved when a woman who had been a waitress and then a manager at My Brothers Bar for thirty-two years was able to convince her son, who happened to own a software company, to purchase the place and keep all these traditions alive. Her son, Danny, had spent time at the bar since he was six years old when his mom began her waitressing job. There are no plans to add a sign or TV, and the Girl Scout cookies will always be available. It's going to remain a family place open from 11:00 to 2:00 am every day, except Sundays, of course.

A Canadian fellow was having a drink in a rough-and-tumble saloon in rural Kentucky.

The bartender said to the fellow, "You're new here. Where are you from?"

The guy answered, "Canada."

The bartender said, "Never been there. What do you do up there?"

"I'm a taxidermist."

Bartender: "A what? Do you drive a taxi?"

"No, I mount animals," the guy replied.

The bartender turned and announced to the crowd. "Relax boys, he's one of us."

Mc Sorley's occupies the ground floor of a five-story, red brick tenement at 15 E 7th Street just off Cooper Square in lower Manhattan. It opened in 1854 and is supposedly the oldest saloon in New York City. Founded by an Irish immigrant, John McSorley, who died in 1910 at the age of 87, the pub is copied after a pub John knew in his hometown, Omagh, Ireland.

No ladies were ever allowed in McSorley's. "Old John" did not believe men could peacefully drink in the presence of women. Should a woman come in, John would hurry forward and say very politely, "Madam, I'm sorry, but we don't serve ladies." If the woman persisted, John would take her by the arm and escort her out the door. This approach lasted a lot longer than you might imagine until August 11th, 1970, when it fell victim to the women's liberation movement. On that date, the New York Daily News ran a photo and headline story about the event. No lady's restroom was available until 1986, sixteen years later.

Another peculiarity of McSorley's is that nothing but light or dark ale has ever been sold there to this day. Once again, Old John felt that no man needed drink stronger than a mug of ale warmed on the hob of a stove. He once said the motto of his saloon should be "good ale, raw onions, and no ladies."

Olde John was an avid collector of memorabilia. Eventually, he managed to cover every square inch of wall space between the wainscot and the ceiling with pictures and souvenirs, and most were still in good condition. There are portraits of Lincoln, Garfield, Kennedy, and McKinley -- all assassinated presidents. There are front pages of old newspapers describing historic events ranging from the London Times article on June 22nd, 1815, an article commenting on the Battle of Waterloo, and another from the New York Herald, April 15th, 1865, which has a one-column story on the shooting of Abraham Lincoln. There is a "wanted poster" for the assassin of Lincoln. There is also a special photo of Babe Ruth saying farewell to Yankee Stadium. It was donated by the photographer, a regular customer.

Another custom of McSorley's was no fixed closing time. When Olde John, and later, his son Bill, felt sleepy, they would summon everyone to the bar and buy a final round.

The bar is very short, accommodating only about five drinkers, and there are no bar stools. Thanks to a succession of owners, little has changed at McSorley's Old Ale House today. There's sawdust on the floor, cash only, no cash register, there never was one. It's a saloon from 200 years ago. During World War One, McSorley's began a tradition of offering a free Turkey dinner and mugs of ale to doughboys departing for France and the war. The guys would hang the turkey wishbones from a gas lamp behind the bar as a good luck wish that they would return. A lot of the wishbones are still hanging there.

As you enter, the bar is on the right, and on the left, there is a row of armchairs with their stiff backs up against the wainscoting. Down the center of the room is a row of old tables. In the middle stands the coal-fired stove with its isinglass door; it still works, and it's still red hot in the winter. In the back room, there are three big dining tables. The attraction is a large painting of a corpulent nude woman stretched out on a couch playing with a parrot hanging right next to a portrait of Peter Cooper, the founder of nearby Cooper Union College. For over 100 years, this was the only woman in the place. The kitchen is in one corner of the room. The food, as it has always been, is simple: hamburgers, hot dogs, sauerkraut, potatoes, and onions. It's good, and it's reasonable.

The regular neighborhood crowd starts showing up by mid-morning. Most come in every day. Some sit by the window and watch the world go by, others read a newspaper, and still others doze off for an hour or two -- this is an old-style saloon. As the day goes on, staff from Bellevue Hospital stop by as well as students from Cooper Union College. By evening, the place is full of a mixture of regulars and an endless parade of tourists.

McSorley's is very well known due to the many photographs and paintings of the place. John Sloan, between 1912 and 1930, did many sketches of McSorley's and five paintings, which have become quite famous. One titled "McSorley's Saturday Night" depicts Bill, Olde John's son, passing out mugs of beer to a crowd of rollicking customers. Another well-known one shows a group of working-class men gathered around the glowing stove with their mugs of ale.

McSorley's did not miss a beat during prohibition. McSorley's ale was produced in the basement in rows and rows of barrels. A retired Brewer from the Bronx would arrive three times a week to make the brew. McSorley's operated for all thirteen years of Prohibition. No passwords or peepholes, everyone was welcome; thanks to Tammany Hall politicians and friendly cops on the beat, McSorley's was never even raided or closed.

In 2001, Joseph Mitchell, a writer with The New Yorker, published a book titled "McSorley's Wonderful Saloon" which does an excellent job of describing the history of this place. Today, McSorley's still opens before noon and closes at 1:00 AM. You can have an ale in the same place where a few presidents enjoyed one back in the 19th century. Ulysses Grant, Abraham Lincoln, and

Teddy Roosevelt have all had a mug at the old Irish saloon. Abraham Lincoln stopped by in 1860 after giving a speech close by at Cooper Union College. It's doubtful he had an ale because he was a lifelong "teetotaler." The current slogan for McSorley's will certainly apply. "We were here before you were born." You probably won't be asked to honor the tradition of urinating on the wall outside -- men only!

CHAPTER 2

For anyone interested in America's history, the Warren Tavern in Charlestown, Massachusetts, is a wonderful example of a colonial tavern. It is named for Doctor Joseph Warren, a leading figure at the beginning of the American Revolution.

Doctor Warren was a Harvard graduate and one of the strongest patriots leading the revolutionary cause in Boston. He was a member of the Sons of Liberty and the Boston Committee of Correspondence. Doctor Warren was the person responsible for sending Paul Revere on his famous ride to warn the colonial militia about the impending British invasion. Doctor Warren was offered a Commission as a Major General. He declined and asked to join the men as a volunteer wherever the fighting was heaviest. The first two British assaults on Bunker Hill were repulsed with heavy British casualties from sniper fire on Charlestown Heights. The British ordered incendiary cannon balls from ships in the harbor to fire on Charlestown, which burned it to the ground since almost all the structures were wooden. During the third assault on Bunker Hill, a British soldier recognized Doctor Warren as one of the revolutionary leaders and shot him in the head, killing him instantly. Remember, in the 1700s warfare was a close-up and personal business. A group of British soldiers took further revenge on Warren and stabbed the body beyond recognition. In remembering Dr. Warren, who was a large loss to the patriots, one military historian, Ethan Refuge, wrote, "No man, with the exception of Samuel Adams, did as much to bring about the rise of a movement powerful enough to lead the people of Massachusetts to revolution."

Five years later, in 1780, Captain Elijah Pellett Newell built the first building in Charlestown following the fire and named the tavern after his good friend and fellow soldier. Now, 243 years later, the tavern is open for business, serving food and drinks, and boasts a record for being the longest-running tavern in Boston.

The Tavern is typical of the era with a low beam ceiling, folks were shorter, and a huge fireplace. Many of Warren's friends visited the Tavern, including Paul Revere, Benjamin Franklin, and George Washington.

You can stop into the Warren Tavern today, open till 1am, and sit and have a drink and make a toast right where these famous patriots once enjoyed a similar drink or two. It is located very close to Boston's Freedom Trail and the historic Bunker Hill site at 2 Pleasant Street.

Fraunces Tavern is still operating at its original location, 54 Pearl Street, corner of Broad, in downtown Manhattan. Built by the DeLancy family in 1719, this place has been a private residence, a hotel, and one of the most important taverns of the Revolutionary War. It is simply brimming with history.

In 1762, Samuel Fraunces purchased the property at fifty-four Pearl Street. They opened it as a tavern, the Queen's Head, and it instantly became a major attraction. It was the regular meeting place for the New York City Chamber of Commerce, Friendly Brothers of Saint Patrick, Knights of the Order of Corsica, and the New York chapter of the Sons of Liberty.

Beginning in 1775, Fraunces Tavern began to get involved in the Revolution. The New York Provincial Congress was founded in the Tavern's Long Room.

In August 1775, the British ship HMS Asia, moored in New York harbor, bombarded the city from midnight until 3am. One of the 18-pound cannonballs from Asia crashed through the roof of the Tavern.

On June 18th, 1776, the Provincial Congress hosted a banquet for General Washington and his staff and officers to express their gratitude for the defense of the colony. It must have been quite a party. There were thirty-one toasts, a fife and drum corps making music, and everyone singing campaign songs. The final bill was 90 pounds, which included 78 bottles of Madeira wine,30 bottles of Port, and 16 shillings for "wine glasses broken."

The British surrendered at Yorktown in October 1781. The British did not leave New York until November 25, 1783-- known as "evacuation day." George Washington led his Continental Army in a parade from Bulls Head Tavern in the Bowery down Broadway to Wall Street and a huge celebration at Fraunces Tavern. Washington remained in New York for the rest of the week, using the Tavern as his headquarters.

On December 4th, 1783, nine days after the last British soldiers left for England, George Washington hosted in the Long Room, his famous farewell party for the officers of the Continental Army. The party began at noon and was a very emotional event; toasting with a glass of wine raised high, Washington addressed the group, "With a heart full of love and gratitude, I now take leave of you. I most devoutly wish that your latter days may be as prosperous and happy as your former ones have been glorious and honorable." This was followed by an overwhelming scene of sadness, sorrow, and weeping.

Samuel Fraunces rendered such aid to the Revolution, especially supplying food to prisoners held by the British in New York City, that after the war, the Continental Congress gave him a special vote of thanks and 200 pounds, a considerable sum at the time.

Following the war, as New York grew, Fraunces Tavern continued to be the major gathering place for important events. On July 4th, 1804, the Society of Cincinnati held a meeting at the Tavern attended by Alexander Hamilton and Aaron Burr, just one week before their famous duel.

Several fires almost destroyed the building in 1832, 1837, and 1852. Major remodeling took place after each fire, and by 1900, the place was almost demolished for new construction. Fortunately, the Daughters of the American Revolution, DAR, saved it.

In 1907, Fraunces Tavern was reconstructed exactly as the original and is considered New York's oldest building on its original site. Today, a museum occupies the second floor, and the building is on the National Register of Historic Places. The Tavern is a tourist site and part of the American Whiskey Trail and the New York Freedom Trail. The Tavern offers the Independence Bar with brunch, lunch, and dinner menus, the Talmadge Room for dining, and the Hideout Bar for private affairs. All rooms offer beer, wine, and cocktails and a generous serving of American history. Finally, there is also a piano bar upstairs.

The City Tavern is an exact replica of the 18th-century building that stood on this site. It is located at 138 S 2nd Street near Independence Hall in Philadelphia. The original building was demolished, and the current structure was opened in 1976 for the American bicentennial celebration.

The first City Tavern was completed in 1774 and was owned by a group of seven wealthy local businessmen. Leading up to the American Revolution, many important meetings took place at the Tavern. John Adams from Boston considered the City Tavern "the most genteel tavern in America." Almost every one of the founding fathers stayed at the City Tavern in the years leading up to the revolution. Members of both the first and second continental congresses also stayed at the Tavern.

Following the passage of the Boston port bill in 1774, over 200 men gathered at the Tavern to respond to a request for assistance from the Bostonians.

City Tavern was the political, social, and business center of the new country, The United States. Jefferson, Adams, Franklin, and Paul Revere all met and ate here. Historians claim the Declaration of Independence and the Constitution both owe much to the beverages and food served in this building.

Following the Revolution, the first celebration of the 4th of July was held at the Tavern in 1777. The same year, George Washington met the Marquis de Lafayette for the first time at the Tavern.

Normally the City Tavern operates as a functioning typical Tavern of the late 1700s, serving beverages and food from recipes of the period. The Tavern closed during the pandemic, 2021-- 2022, and it has not re-opened.

In 2022, one of the delightful old neighborhood bars on Chicago's near north side was being torn down for another new high rise. The workmen found a human skeleton standing perfectly upright between the joists behind a wall. All work had to cease until the medical examiner determined the identity of the body. After much examination, it turned out to be Stan Kowalski, the 1997 Polish neighborhood "Hide and Seek" champion.

Most of the places mentioned in this book continue to operate in the original building at the original location. Because of their very special historical significance to our country, the following taverns are authentic recreations. Thanks to the philanthropy of John D Rockefeller Jr. during the 1930s, the town of Williamsburg, Virginia, has been recreated to appear exactly as it did in the middle 1700s when it was the capital of colonial Virginia. Williamsburg played a significant role in the years leading up to the American Revolution. It was in the taverns of Williamsburg that the patriots George Washington, Thomas Jefferson, Patrick Henry, George Mason, and others met periodically to discuss problems with the British Tea Act, the Townsend Act, the Intolerable Acts, and other injustices. The Duke of Gloucester Street is lined with fully and carefully restored taverns and other buildings of the period. President Franklin Roosevelt called it "the most historic street in America." All the taverns are open for touring, and several are operating as they did in the 1770s, serving the same food and drink as the colonists ate: peanut soup, fried chicken, potato dumplings, spoon bread, crab cakes, oysters, mussels, and cider.

Christiana Campbell's Tavern is a wonderful example of an operating Tavern. Located at 101 South Waller Street, Just off Duke of Gloucester, the Tavern opened in 1775 when Christiana Campbell returned to Williamsburg with her two daughters and opened the Tavern to support her family after her husband had died. She was familiar with the tavern business because her father had operated one in Williamsburg near the capital for many years.

Campbell advertised her establishment as "a genteel Tavern offering class accommodations and the very best seafood and entertainment." She was targeting the upper class to avoid price limits on food and lodging established for regular taverns by the local government. The many ledgers of George Washington housed in the Library of Congress show he was a frequent overnight guest at Christiana Campbell's Tavern. As the war approached, he was often joined by Thomas Jefferson. It is wonderful that today, you can walk into Christiana Campbell's Tavern, an exact replica of the original, have a drink, and order from the same menu as the one used by the Patriots almost 300 years ago. Oysters were Washington's favorite!

Once the war began, business declined, and the capital moved to Richmond in 1780, so Christiana Campbell sold the business and moved to live with her daughters in Fredericksburg, VA.

William and Mary College, founded in 1694, is the second oldest College in America and is located next to the restored town. The Raleigh Tavern, also located on Duke of Gloucester Street, is fully restored and open for visitors. It does not serve food nor drinks. The Apollo Room of the Raleigh Tavern is especially famous for key meetings of the elected officials of Virginia and the resulting decisions to participate in the Revolution. The Apollo room is also famous as where William and Mary's students established Phi Beta Kappa, the scholastic honorary society, in 1776.

The Wayside Inn is located on the old Boston Post Road in Sudbury, Massachusetts, halfway between Worcester and Boston. This historic landmark opened in 1686 and is still in operation over 300 years later. There aren't many structures in America still standing and in use after 300 years; fire, urban growth, and demolition usually take their toll. The Wayside Inn had a devastating fire in December 1955, but the careful restoration includes much of the original building.

The fame of the Wayside Inn, in addition to its age, dates from 1862, when the poet Henry Wadsworth Longfellow visited the inn with his publisher, James T Fields, when it was named the Red Horse Tavern. Shortly afterward, Longfellow began to compile his poems using the inn as the setting. The final book published in 1863 using the title, "Tales of a Wayside Inn," presents a series of stories told by different guests at the Inn.

The collection of poems became a major hit across America. The next year, the Wayside Inn became "Longfellow's Wayside Inn" in order to capitalize on all the publicity, even though Longfellow had never stayed there overnight.

Henry Wadsworth Longfellow was born in 1807 in Portsmouth, Maine, and graduated from Bowden College, where he later became a professor. By 1847, when "Evangeline" was published, Longfellow was well-known and a very successful individual. "Evangeline" remains one of the most popular poems in the world. It is a story based on a girl searching for her lover. Acadians had been separated when the British deported them to Louisiana from Nova Scotia. Another extremely popular work of Longfellow's is "The Song of Hiawatha," published in 1855. This is an American Indian love story.

Longfellow was struck by tragedy in 1861 before he visited the Tavern when his wife was killed in an accidental fire. She was at her desk sealing envelopes with hot wax when her clothes caught on fire. Longfellow was asleep but awakened and attempted to save her. His burns to the face left heavy scarring, which is why he wore what became a trademark beard for the rest of his life. Longfellow was depressed and suffering from "writer's block" when he wrote the "Tales of a Wayside Inn," and this is reflected in some of the stories. The opening lines, "Listen My Children, and

You Shall Hear the Midnight Ride of Paul Revere," remain popular to this day.

Longfellow never fully recovered from his wife's death and remained depressed, lonely, and withdrawn for the rest of his life. His popularity was immense both here in the U.S. and abroad. A collection of his poems sold 10,000 copies on the first day of sales in London. By 1855, he had resigned from both teaching jobs at Bowden and Harvard and devoted his time fully to writing. He was so popular that his 70th birthday in 1877 was celebrated around the Country like a national holiday with parades, speeches, fireworks, and readings of his work.

Longfellow passed away in 1882 at the age of 75 at home in Cambridge, Massachusetts. The Wayside Inn had several owners from 1862 until Henry Ford, the industrialist, purchased it in 1923 along with 3000 acres surrounding the Inn. Ford's plan was to create a historic village and museum. This plan never happened, and Ford directed his efforts and wealth toward creating the Greenfield Village in Dearborn, Michigan. The Ford foundation did fully restore the Wayside Inn following the fire in 1955. Ford also created the Wayside Inn Foundation, a nonprofit that oversees the Inn and adjacent 100 acres and nine restored buildings as a U. S. Historical site.

Today, the Wayside Inn is the oldest operating inn on the oldest commissioned road, Old Boston Post Rd, in the United States. Ten historically accurate rooms are available for rent. The restaurant offers breakfast, lunch, and dinner, and the bar is open for your enjoyment. The bar is on the right as you walk in the front door. This is the landmark bar where Lieutenant Colonel Ezekiel Howe toasted his fellow Revolutionaries with a drink of ale before he led the contingent to Concord on April 19th, 1775, when the Revolutionary War began. Paul Revere's ride from Boston to Lexington to warn the patriots the "British are coming" took place at midnight on April 18th, 1775.

Two guys sitting at the bar have been drinking for a while. One says, "Tell me, after you've had a couple of martinis does your penis burn?" Other fellow answers, "I don't know, never tried to light it."

The Stork Club was a nightclub in Manhattan, and during its existence, from 1928 to 1965, it was the most famous night spot in the world. Even though it has been closed since 1965, I decided to include a description because it was such a once-in-a-lifetime, special bar. At the time, there were plenty of bars, clubs, and saloons; it was estimated that New York City had 1100 night clubs in 1945, one-third of the US total. The Stork Club was a 20th-century symbol of "cafe society"; the really wealthy elite, including movie stars, athletes, celebrities, showgirls, and aristocrats. They were all together every night in the VIP Cub Room of the Stork Club.

The Stork Club was owned and operated by Sherman Billingsly, an ex-bootlegger from Enid, Oklahoma. The first Stork Club opened in 1929 on West 58th Street. The story is Billingsley was contacted in his real estate office, which was nearby, by two gamblers that he knew back in Oklahoma. These gentlemen offered to finance Billingsley in opening a New York club. The club was raided a couple of times during the Prohibition years and eventually reopened in 1934 at 3 E. 53rd Street, where it remained until it closed in October 1965.

Other New York nightclubs had their special base; Toots Shore's was the sports hangout, and El Morocco attracted a sophisticated audience. However, the Stork Club mixed power, money, and glamour.

In the early days, Billingsley's Oklahoma partners sold their share of the business to a group of New York mobsters from the Costello mafia family. Shortly afterward, Billingsley was kidnapped by a rival gang and held for ransom. The individual sent to collect the ransom money was lured to a phone booth and shot to death. Following all the publicity of this event, Billingsley's mob partners decided to sell out, and Sherman bought the whole business, including the building.

One of the things that made the Stork Club so popular was the constant stream of publicity it received in the 14 daily New York newspapers. This was the era of the newspaper gossip columnist, and Walter Winchell made the Stork Club his nightly headquarters. He had his own corner table, #50, where he would not only gather material for the next day's column but he would also broadcast his nationwide nightly radio show.

With the celebrity crowd it attracted, of course, many famous events and plenty of scandals took place at the Stork Club. It counted among its frequent guests the Kennedy and Roosevelt families and the Duke and Duchess of Windsor. The news of Grace Kelly's engagement to Prince Rainier of Monaco was announced while they were visiting the Stork Club; the wealthy socialite Evelyn Walsh McLean, who owned the 45-carat Hope diamond and would often wear it, lost the gem under the table at the Club one evening. So many people were on the floor looking for it, it took a while to find it.

Ernest Hemingway, who seemed to be everywhere, arrived one evening showing off the $100,000 check he had received for the movie rights to his novel "For Whom the Bell Tolls." Hemingway challenged Billingsley to cash it to settle his bill. Billingsley told him to wait till closing at 4am, and he would gladly handle it.

Most of the big night spots had a regular feature attraction, Frank Sinatra, Perry Como, or Louis Armstrong. The Stork Club decided their clientele was the only feature they needed. There was a band nightly that offered music for dancing in the main dining room, but the place to be was in the famous "VIP Cub Room." Billingsley had constructed a large private room intended for his private use. The room became the "place" to be in this huge club. The Stork Club welcomed over 2500 "guests" a night and grossed over seventeen million dollars annually in today's money. Being invited to the Cub Room was a big deal. The large guy handling the door was nicknamed "Saint Peter."

During World War II, the Stork Club became so well known that US Eighth Air Force bombers were emblazoned with the club emblem, a top-hatted pink stork. In 1945, a full-length feature movie titled *The Stork Club* debuted, starring Barry Fitzgerald, Barbara Hutton, and Robert Benchley. The plot of the film was based on life at the Club. The Club even had its own weekly TV show beginning in 1950 with Sherman Billingsley interviewing celebrities at Stork Club tables.

The Stork Club reached its peak in the 50s, but society changed a lot when the 1960s arrived, and it closed its doors in October 1965. Most of the New York clubs had become unionized, but Billingsley would never give in to the labor unions. As a result, there was frequent nighttime picketing that went on for years. Many of the Club's regular patrons did not like dealing with these confrontations. Many observers trace the decline to the day John Kennedy was assassinated. Jack and Jackie were long-time patrons of the Stork Club. It was never the same after that tragedy. Sherman Billingsley, convicted bootlegger and nightclub owner extraordinaire, was in "his club" every single evening of his life, and he never drank alcohol. He died exactly one year after the club closed, October 1966, at age seventy. The Stork Club, where all those wonderful times prevailed, became a public park. It's too bad we can't go back and visit this bar where so many famous people enjoyed themselves.

Lady Astor and Winston Churchill had a rivalry that included trading incriminating, sarcastic comments. Churchill was commenting aloud about what to wear to the annual parliamentary costume party. Lady Astor, whom Churchill loved to call Nancy, said, "Why don't you go sober? Nobody will recognize you!"

CHAPTER 3

England is the home of the pub, short for public house, and there are over 40,000 throughout the Country. The pub has been a very important part of British life for hundreds of years, especially in the smaller country villages. One of the oldest and most interesting is the *Eagle Pub*, located on Benay Street on the campus of the famous Cambridge University in the center of the city. The Eagle opened in 1667 as a coaching inn accommodating guests on the London stagecoach route.

During the Second World War, the landscape around Cambridge was dotted with air bases. There was one located on average every eight miles. The Eagle became a favorite spot for off-duty Royal Air Force personnel to unwind from the stress of flying sorties over Nazi Germany. A small room at the rear of the pub is known as the RAF Bar. The walls are completely covered with photographs of planes and the smiling, young, leather-jacketed guys who flew them. Flying the Lancaster bomber on the nightly raids over heavily fortified German territory was extremely dangerous duty; the casualty rate was very high. The RAF Bomber Command lost over 55,000 young men during the war. There are many mementos from the war decorating the bar: gasoline cans, flying boots, sunglasses, pairs of gloves, etc.

The special attraction is the ceiling, where every inch is covered with names, initials, squadron numbers, girlfriend's names, and almost anything else you can imagine. A flight Sergeant by the name of P. E. Turner was the first to climb atop a table one night and burn his squadron number into the plaster using a cigarette lighter. It did not take long for others to add their mark using lighted candles, knives, and even the girl's lipstick. By 1987, over forty years later, the ceiling had become soiled and faded, and plans were made to repaint it. Thanks to one person, a regular patron named James Cheney, who spotted something interesting while gazing at the ceiling, the ceiling was carefully cleaned, and Cheney set about to record every inscription left by these brave men. Today, there is a document placed on one of the walls that records sixty-four RAF squadrons, names, or numbers of several of the planes, and the identification of many of the RAF Flyers. What a wonderful place, 400 years old, and now partially a museum, but you can still sit down in the RAF Bar and take pride in offering a toast to these heroes that helped save us from Nazi fascism and managed to decorate the ceiling of a bar.

The Eagle Pub is very famous for another incident that took place there. The Cambridge University eminent Cavendish Experimental Physics Laboratory, founded in 1874, occupied buildings across the street from the Eagle Pub. The pub was a favorite luncheon and "end of the day" hang out for the scientists and staff of the laboratory. The Cavendish labs are given credit for an extraordinary number of scientific achievements over the years, including the discovery of the electron and the neutron, the first controlled artificial nuclear fusion, the cloud chamber, and advanced uses of the electron microscope. Scientists at the lab have been awarded 32 Nobel prizes for their many achievements in physics, biology, and medicine.

February 28th, 1953, one of the physicists, Francis Crick, came into the Eagle pub at lunchtime and dramatically announced that using the electron microscope, he and James Watson had discovered "the secret of life." They had been able to identify the double Helix structure of DNA. This explains how DNA carries genetic information. This was a major biological discovery, and Crick and Watson received the Nobel Prize in 1962; also, in 1953, during lunch at the Pub, Crick, and Watson were able to draw up a list of the 20 catatonic amino acids that are key to understanding the protein coating nature of DNA.

A major part of the Cavendish Laboratories moved to new quarters in 1974. The Eagle Pub, now owned by the University, remains a popular destination for the lab employees. So here is a 400-year-old pub where you can go today, anytime between 11am and 11pm, and not only have a pub lunch, but you can probably strike up a conversation with some really intelligent people.

The Grenadier Pub, located in the Belgravia section of London near Hyde Park and Buckingham Palace, has all the ingredients of a wonderful British pub. It's old, charming, haunted, overflowing with history, and still serving food and ale every day. It's probably London's most famous pub.

Built in 1720 in a courtyard on the grounds of the home of the First Regiment of the First Guards, an elite unit of the British Army, it was the mess hall for the senior officers of the unit. Officers of the Duke of Wellington's army on leave from fighting Napoleon at the battle of Waterloo across the English Channel in Belgium returned to drink and play Skittles in the basement of the Grenadier. The original pewter bar and the Skittles games are still there, and the walls are covered with memorabilia.

The Battle of Waterloo between the French and a combination of Prussian and British armies led by the Duke of Wellington took place on Sunday, June 18th, 1815. It was the decisive battle of the age. There were 50,000 casualties plus 7000 horses: very high for the weapons available at the time. The battle ranks as one of history's major turning points. The one-day, nine-hour battle was decided when the Prussian army arrived midafternoon and attacked the French flank. The battle brought to an end twenty-three continuous years of war on the European continent. Napoleon abdicated his throne four days after the battle, and that ended France's bid to dominate Europe. Over four decades of peace resulted from this one battle. Waterloo is directly across the English Channel, only about thirty-five miles from downtown London.

The ceiling of the pub is totally covered with banknotes and bills of various currencies, two and three deep in many spots. Two hundred years is a long time for visitors to be sticking bills to the ceiling of a pub. The story behind this tradition involves a young enlisted man in the Guards who was caught cheating at cards one evening and beaten to death. This supposedly occurred in September, and the ghost of the young man has haunted the pub ever since, especially during September. The purpose of the money stuck to the ceiling is hopefully to pay off the ghost's debts so he will finally leave. Some London financial experts feel there is enough money stuck to the ceiling to start a small savings and loan bank. The officer's club became a public house pub in 1818. It was named the Grenadier in honor of the regiment's valor at Waterloo.

So, think about it, you can take a 12-minute walk from Harrod's Department Store, go down a couple cobblestone alleys, go in, order lunch and an ale, sit down, and be where the Duke of Wellington and his officers celebrated one of the world's major victories a little over 200 years ago. Open from 12 noon to 11pm every day, serving lunch and dinner and plenty of beer and ale.

Lady Astor was giving one of her many speeches lamenting the curse of drinking alcohol. At one point, she exclaims, "My God in heaven, I would rather commit adultery than have whiskey touch my lips." A loud voice from the rear shouted, "Who wouldn't?"

The bar at the Connaught Hotel in London's Mayfair district is the only bar to win the coveted "best bar in the world" title more than once. It manages to finish in the top 10 every year. The best bar award is given annually by "the world's 50 best bars" panel of over 500 judges. The Connaught has also received the *Europe's Best Bar* award several years in a row.

The Connaught Hotel, built in 1897, has been a favorite of the rich and famous ever since. Sir Alec Guinness, an actor, had a suite reserved at the Connaught, where he stayed for 30 years when in London between 1970 and 2000. Rooms at the Connaught cost about $1200 a night.

The whole place reeks of upper class, and the bar shouts glamor. The style, known as *cubist art*, of the 1920s includes textured walls adorned with platinum silver leaf, overstuffed leather chairs, huge mirrors, and candles on the tables. The bartenders are known as *mixologists*.

The Connaught is known for its signature drink, the dry martini, often considered the world's most famous drink. The drink is prepared at your table from the martini trolley, a sleek black lacquered trolley with four wheels holding all the necessary ingredients to produce the world's best martini. The recipe converted from the metric system is the following: 2.4 ounces of High Claire Castle gin or Snow Queen vodka, .5 ounces of vermouth, 3 dashes of bitters, choice of three varieties. Add the bitters to a frosted martini glass, stir the gin or vodka vigorously with chunks of ice in a mixing glass, and pour into the etched crystal martini glass from a height. Add lemon or olive, and serve straight up. This will cost you about thirty dollars, but you will be drinking it in a prestigious place with a clientele to match. Open every day from 4pm to 1am.

A few random comments about the British and martinis. When Winston Churchill drank martinis, not often, his favorite was made with Plymouth gin and served at Donovan's Bar in the Brown Hotel in downtown London. In a bit of sarcasm from World War II, the British like to refer to a very, very dry martini as a "Montgomery." This refers to British general Bernard Montgomery, who apparently preferred an advantage in troop ratio of seventeen to one before ordering an attack on the enemy.

The famous British spy of fiction and films, James Bond, preferred dry martinis. In the now famous line from the movie "Goldfinger," Bond orders "a martini, shaken not stirred." It turns out that the author, Ian Fleming, likes martinis and always felt stirring a drink diminished the flavor. In the 14 novels, beginning in 1973, James Bond appears to drink equal numbers of gin or vodka martinis.

London has a lot of pubs, and many of them include a lot of history. The Prospect of Whitby is a public house on the banks of the Thames River at Wapping in the London borough of Tower of Hamlets. It includes a beer garden and claims to be the oldest Riverside Tavern, dating to 1520. The Tavern was once known as the Devil's Tavern on account of its dubious reputation. Historically, all that remains from the original building is the 400-

year-old stone floor, 18th-century wall paneling, and the 19th-century facade. Inside, there is a pewter top bar, and the decorations include many nautical items collected from the years catering to sailors, pirates, smugglers, cutthroats, and an endless stream of undesirables.

In the 17th century, it became the hangout for "hanging judge" George Jeffries. George Jeffries was a Welsh judge who became notable during the reign of King James the Second, 1685-1688, rising to the position of Lord Chancellor. His job was to enforce royal policy, and he built a reputation for severity and bias. After a revolt known as the Monmouth Rebellion, Jeffries is credited with sentencing over 700 rebels to death by hanging. This is where he acquired the nickname.

Judge Jeffries lived near the Tavern, and it was his custom after sentencing people to sit by the window, have a drink, a little lunch, and watch the hangings at the nearby execution dock. The procedure required hanging at low tide and remaining hanging until three tides had overflowed the body. These were public hangings and served as entertainment at the time, as well as a lesson. Often, the prisoners were simply tied to a stake and left until the tide drowned them.

A replica of the gallows and noose stands outside the pub window to commemorate Judge Jeffries' custom and the pub's infamous customer. Jeffries finally met his end in 1688 when King James was ousted, and Jeffries had to run for his life disguised as a sailor. Eventually caught, he was so hated that the new regime put him in the Tower of London for his own safety. He died there in 1688 of kidney disease.

Following a serious fire in the early 19th century, the pub was rebuilt and renamed the Prospect of Whitby. The name came from a coal freighter that used to dock frequently next to the pub as it brought coal from Newcastle to London.

Many scenes of the pub were painted by both Whistler and Turner. The pub has been featured in movies and TV shows, especially "D-Day, the 6th of June" starring Robert Taylor and Richard Todd. Over the centuries, famous people from Charles Dickens to Princess Margaret to Richard Burton and Prince Rainier have been "regulars" at the Prospect of Whitby. It's open every day till 11pm, serving traditional pub snacks and regular meals. Be sure to get a window seat and enjoy the view!

The Olde Cheshire Cheese Pub at 145 Fleet Street in London, England, sits on the site of a 13th-century Carmelite monastery. Since 1538, a pub has occupied this spot. The current medieval pub was rebuilt in 1667 after the "Great Fire of London" in 1666.

The sign for the pub reads "Ye Olde Cheshyre Cheese," and the place is especially noteworthy for the number of prominent literary figures who were regular patrons. The location on Fleet Street, in the center of London's historic publishing district, made it a hub for literary types. You can sit at a long oak table in the dining room used hundreds of years ago by Charles Dickens, WB Yates, Mark Twain, Alfred Tennyson, and Arthur Conan Doyle. Doctor Samuel Johnson, the author of the precursor to the modern dictionary, lived just a few doors away. His table and chair are still in the pub, and you can visit his house a few steps down the street. The place is featured in Charles Dickens' novel "A Tale of Two Cities." Oliver Goldsmith lived next door. Dickens describes their drinking and dining at the pub in the "Tale of Two Cities."

The old Cheshire pub is big and has a labyrinth of rooms: First bar room, Chop House restaurant, Cheshire bar, Cellar bar, and several more named rooms. There are many photos and mementos throughout the pub to add to its historical significance. The Function Room dates from the 17th century and has an impressive ceiling with oaken beams that go all the way to the roof. The room is available for large events, weddings, reunions, anniversaries etcetera.

Polly, a parrot, lived at the pub for forty years. She entertained princes, celebrities, and visitors from around the world. When Polly died in 1926, the obituary appeared in over 200 newspapers around the world and was broadcast on the BBC network. The stuffed Poly is on display near the entrance to the pub.

The Olde Cheshire Cheese likes to boast it is probably the "most famous pub in the world." No doubt it is a very special place. There is still sawdust spread on the floor twice a day. You can dine on good pub fare in wooden bays with high-backed church pews for seating. It is almost 400 years old and is open daily from noon to 11 pm.

A Scotchman entered a pub outside London and immediately ordered drinks for "the house." The bartender said, "Boy, we're pretty crowded. You must be celebrating something big to buy everyone a drink." The Scotchman says, "Big? I guess so, my wife just gave birth to a 25-pound baby boy." Well, everyone was celebrating, but *nobody could believe a 25-pound baby. A few weeks later, the Scotchman returned to the bar. The bartender was anxious to find out how the baby was doing. Scotsman says, "Oh, he's just great, weighs fourteen pounds," the bartender says. "I thought he weighed twenty-five pounds when he was born." "Well, we had him circumcised."*

The Globe Inn is located at 56 High Street in Dumfries, Scotland, and is a wonderful example of an old Scottish pub. By old, we mean established in 1610. There's a lot of history built into the Globe. Dumfries is about thirty-five minutes from Glasgow and two hours from Edinburgh.

Robert Burns, Scotland's national poet, spent eight years in Dumfries from 1788 to 1796, when he worked part-time as an excise tax collector to supplement the income from his farm outside of town. The Globe became Burn's favorite haunt, and he spent many evenings with friends in the backroom enjoying a few glasses of claret and discussing the politics of the day and the many songs and poems he had written. Everyone spent time reading the daily newspapers delivered by the Stagecoach with news of the French Revolution. Many times, the volume of tax work required him to be in Dumfries for several days, and on these occasions, he lodged at the Globe. In the upstairs bedroom, where he spent many an evening working on his tax ledgers and his poetry, he also had time to inscribe six different verses on the window pane using a diamond tip stylus. All of this can still be seen today in the same restored bedroom over 200 years later.

Burns was a young man in his early thirties, and on these extended periods away from home, he had an affair with Anne Park, the nineteen-year-old niece of Mrs. Hyslop, the landlady of the Inn. Anne was from Edinburgh and worked as a barmaid at the Globe. She was a very attractive blonde young lady. Burns began writing songs and poems about Anne, and it didn't take long before she was pregnant. Anne returned to Edinburgh to have the baby. When Burns' wife Jean found out about the situation, she raised the little girl as one of her own.

The chair that Burns used during his stays at the Globe is still there and is known as the "poet's chair." You can actually sit in it, but you must be able to recite at least one line of Burns' poetry or pay the penalty of buying a round of drinks for the "house."

In 1788, Burns built a barn on his farm, and it was in this barn that he wrote much of his work, including his most famous "Auld Lang Syne," which he wrote in 1788, although it was not published until after his death in 1796. Robert Burns authored a lot of material, but he only lived to be thirty-seven years old. Auld Lang Syne, *Should Old Acquaintance be Forgotten and Never Brought to*

Mind, is the banner New Year's Eve song around the world. He is credited with many more songs, poems, and sayings, including, *The best-laid plans of mice and men often go astray.*

The Globe reopened in July 2021 after a major refurbishing job that preserved most of the Robert Burns artifacts. The original bar room and grand dining room are serving lunch and dinner Tuesday through Saturday with over 300 single malt whiskeys available. Isn't it wonderful this pub has been open for business since 1610!

Patrick was riding his brand-new motorcycle on the road down to Cork City when he came upon his best friend, Mike, walking along the edge of the road. Patrick stopped and said, *"Mike, hop on my new bike, and I'll give you a lift to town." "Thanks, Patrick, but I'm a little afraid of those things, and the wind hits me right in the chest."* Patrick says, *"Oh, Mike, it's beginning to rain. I'll tell you, take your jacket off and hold your arms up. We're going to put your jacket on backwards and zip it up the back. That way, the wind won't be able to get through your jacket." Off they go to Cork, Patrick looks back to see how Mike is doing. He has fallen off the bike, and the crowd has gathered in the road in front of the local pub. Patrick turns the bike around, speeds back to where the crowd has gathered, makes his way through the throng, approaches the spot, and shouts, "It's my pal, Mike. He fell off my bike. How's he doing?" One of the bystanders looks up and says, "he was doing just fine till Seamus here tried to turn his head around."*

Davy Byrnes Pub, Dublin, Ireland

Temple Bar, Dublin, Ireland

Hofbrauhaus, Munich, Germany

Hirshgarten, Munich, Germany

Octoberfest, Munich, Germany

Octoberfest, Munich, Germany

Harry's New York Bar, Paris

Hemingway Bar, Ritz Hotel, Paris

Coca Chanel

Guiseppe Cipriani, Harry's Bar, Venice, Italy

Harry's Bar, Venice, Italy

Bar Marcella, Barcelona, Spain

Bar Marcella, Barcelona, Spain 2

Raffles Hotel, Singapore

The Long Bar, Raffles Hotel, Singapore

Ed White – Minnestoa Vikings

Billy Martin, Yankee Baseball

Bantry, Ireland

Kilgoban Pub, Bantry, Ireland

Ireland has over 7000 pubs, and Dublin alone has over 770 drinking establishments. A unique Irish national holiday is

"Bloomsday," celebrated every June 16th. In the Irish author James Joyce's novel "Ulysses," the entire 700-page story takes place on one day, June 16th, 1904, when Leopold Bloom wanders across Dublin. Bloom's journey includes numerous appointments and stops at the cemetery, the hospital, the pharmacy, and several pubs. On Bloomsday, many fans of James Joyce honor the author by tracing Bloom's steps in 1904. They dress in appropriate costumes for the date, listen to "readings" at various points of interest, and have a drink at the many pubs mentioned in the story. The most popular one and open for business every day is Davy Byrnes, located at 21 Duke Street. It was here that Leopold Bloom stopped for a lunch of gorgonzola cheese and Burgundy wine. In the book, Bloom also gives a glowing description of the bar, the quality of the wood, and the beauty of the shape.

During his Dublin days, James Joyce was a regular at Davie Byrnes Pub because it had a reputation for being Dublin's #1 "Literary Pub," and many well-known authors met there on a regular basis. Davy Byrnes opened in 1798 and became the hangout for writers in the late 1800s. During the "War for Independence," 1919-1922, the pub served a different clientele, and the upstairs room became a headquarters for the revolutionary IRA and one of its leaders, Michael Collins.

Davey Byrnes Pub is mentioned in several of James Joyce's novels and short stories, and he was well acquainted with the owner and namesake. It was the association with the novel "Ulysses" that put it on the map of the "Must visit Pubs." Ulysses was published in 1922, and it was controversial from day one-- banned and censored in many places. Interestingly, Joyce chose June 16th, 1904, as the day for the story. He chose that day because it was the anniversary of the first time he had sex with his future wife, Nora Barnacle.

Today, Ulysses is often declared the greatest novel of the 20th century. If you choose to give it a look, be warned that it is written in Joyce's "Stream of consciousness" style, which can be difficult to handle. It might be easier to pay a visit to Davie Byrne's 200-year-old Irish pub and relax with a wine and something other than a gorgonzola cheese sandwich.

Paddy decided to sneak out of the house and go down to the corner pub for a pint or two. He was really enjoying himself, and closing time had arrived. Paddy made it outside, but the next thing he realized, he was on his hands and knees, unable to stand up. Paddy said to himself, "Boy, I am really drunk. I've got to get home." So, on his hands and knees, poor Paddy crawled all the way home, sneaked into the house, and went to bed. The next morning, the wife wakes Paddy and says, "So you were down to the pub again last night?" Paddy says, "What makes you say that?" The wife says, "They called. You left your wheelchair down there again."

Dublin's Temple Bar, built in 1846, is not the city's oldest or most historical pub. Today, it is certainly the most popular, attracting over three and a half million visitors a year. In the late 19th century, the whole area around the Temple Bar began to deteriorate, and many shops were open during the day. Prostitution and crime took over at night. Over the years, urban decay took its toll, and many buildings began to deteriorate. By 1970, the City made plans to demolish the whole area and build a parking garage and a large bus terminal. Other officials offered a plan to regenerate the area, now known as the Temple Bar neighborhood. People are attracted to the quaint cobblestone pedestrian walkways, the many boutique shops, and two Cultural centers. At night, the area really comes alive with over ten pubs attracting both local folks and visitors. And music is everywhere.

Many famous Irish groups can trace their beginning to the Temple Bar area of Dublin. Bono, of the popular U2 band, owns one of the pubs located in the Temple Bar neighborhood.

At the Temple Bar, in a show of respect to James Joyce, there is a large bronze statue of him inside the front door. The Temple Bar is big, but you will find it crowded. One other attraction, the place offers 450 different whiskeys. Some are quite rare, the most in Ireland. It also claims to offer the world's largest selection of pub sandwiches. The exterior of the Temple Bar is the most photographed pub in the world. Open 10 am. to 1:30 am, later on weekends. And with the reputation for providing wonderful music every day of the week beginning at 10:30 am.

Bob Newhart, the comedian, used to describe his heritage as half German and half Irish. "So, I'm a meticulous drunk."

CHAPTER 4

Unlike the rest of Europe, who prefer to drink in pubs, cafes, and other smaller bars, the Germans prefer to drink beer in big beer halls or huge outdoor beer gardens.

The most famous beer hall in the world is the Hofbräuhaus in Munich, Germany. The name and the beer steins with a distinctive logo have been franchised everywhere. There is even an exact full-size replica of the Hofbräuhaus in Las Vegas.

The Hofbräuhaus and brewery were built by the Bavarian Duke Maximilian in 1589. Bavaria had beers of its own, but they were not very good. So, the Duke decided to build his own brewery and imported people from the North to run it. The duke had a monopoly position for beer production, and the Hofbräuhaus brewery accounted for 50% of Bavaria's state income in the 17th century. It was originally open only to the royalty of Bavaria, and the public was not admitted until King Ludwig came along in 1828.

Allied air raids in World War II pretty well demolished most of Munich, including the Hofbräuhaus. It took over a decade from the end of the war in 1945 until 1958 to reopen.

As you can imagine, after being around for over 400 years, the Hofbräuhaus has some major stories. Wolfgang Amadeus Mozart lived right around the corner from the Hofbräuhaus in the late 18th century. He visited the bar almost on a daily basis. It is claimed that he wrote a poem at the Hofbräuhaus, and after several more visits, he used it to write the opera Ido Meno.

In 1897, the brewery part of the Hofbräuhaus was moved to the suburbs to gain additional space for the restaurant. In the years prior to the First World War, Vladimir Lenin was a frequent patron. He sat at a corner table playing chess. In her diary, Lenin's wife wrote how much she enjoyed the beer and friends at the Hofbräuhaus. The third floor contains the Festival Room, one of the few parts not damaged during the air raids. It was here in 1919 that the Munich Communist Party set up its headquarters. On February 24th, 1920, Adolf Hitler presented the Nazi party's infamous "Twenty-five-point program" in the Festival Room. During Hitler's speech, a riot broke out between the Communists and the Nazis, known as the Social Democrats. Hitler finished his speech amid a chaos of broken tables, chairs, and beer mugs. Many more Nazi party meetings were held in the Festival Room. Hitler returned to the Hofbräuhaus often after gaining power in the 1930s. Hitler was also an artist and did a painting of the exterior of the Hofbräuhaus.

In 1935, William "Waga" Gabriel composed the famous Hofbräuhaus song, "There is a Hofbräuhaus in Munich one, two, down the Hatch." This song remains extremely popular today as a drinking song.

There is ample entertainment at the Hofbräuhaus featuring well-known German "Drinking music." The Hofbräuhaus even has its own currency, beer tokens, which are very popular with the "Regulars." One advantage of the tokens is that they do not fluctuate in value, always good for a liter of beer. Local pensioners in the Munich area often receive a monthly allotment of beer tokens as part of their retirement payment. The Hofbräuhaus is cavernous, and about 35,000 folks visit on an average day, including a lot of regulars. Many of them have their own beer steins stored at the bar in individual lockers in a special "safe room." The steins are available whenever the regulars pay a visit. With crowds like this, you might wonder where to sit and have your beer. Well, you can sit almost anywhere. And don't be shy about joining others at a table. It's the custom in Germany to "move up" and be "cozy." An important rule: "Do not sit at a table that has a sign "Stammtisch" meaning. "Gathering." These tables are by invitation only and belong to the regulars. Over 120 separate organizations hold meetings at the Hofbräuhaus weekly, daily, monthly, or annually.

The Hofbräuhaus, 400 years old, is open for business every day from 9:00am to midnight at Platyl9 in Munich, Germany. Some of the rooms at the Hofbräuhaus require an advance reservation. The Festival Room, for example, the beer hall or the beer garden, does not require reservations.

In addition to the beer hall, Germany's other special drinking attraction is the beer garden. The German beer garden is London's Pub, France's Bistro, or Italy's Cafe. It's not just a place to drink. It's a place to gather with friends, meet new ones, or just rest in the shade, or let the kids play and enjoy lunch or dinner. One major advantage, you can either order food from a large selection or bring your own. Another odd tradition, when it's time to order a beer, you go to the bar and select a Stein from an adjoining cupboard, take it to one of the nearby wash basins, wash it, and return to have it filled.

You won't have any difficulty deciding which beer to drink because each beer garden serves only one of their brands from Munich's six major breweries, all located within the city limits. Although the beer selection is limited, the food choices are extensive. Two popular choices on every menu of every beer garden are pretzel bread with cheese and fish on a stick. No utensils are needed to dine on either one. Since many groups include the whole family, from grandpa and grandson to the little grandchildren, it is wonderful that you are permitted to bring your own food. It's important to have the standard blue and white tablecloth to reserve the table. Blue and white are the Bavarian state colors and are prominently on display everywhere.

Another bit of advice concerns the size of the beer steins. The standard beer stein holds one liter, and one liter is equal to about 34 ounces. The standard-sized beer bottle in the US holds 12 ounces. So, drinking a stein of beer is almost the same as having three bottles of beer. The other thing to remember is the weight of the average Stein empty it is about three pounds. When you see photos of those good-looking German waitresses in their neat costumes carrying three steins of beer in each hand, they are carrying about thirty pounds total. A liter of beer weighs two pounds.

There are over 100 beer gardens in Munich. A favorite and the largest is the Hirschgarten, dating from 1791. The Hirschgarten covers over forty acres of meadowland and is filled with big, old, shady chestnut trees. It has seating for 8,000. And somehow, it's never quite full—there's always room for a newcomer or even a latecomer. An added attraction for families is a wildlife park located next door, where there are always deer wandering through the beer garden. There is also a carousel, a playground for children, and barbecues for cooking.

One other special German drinking venue is the annual Munich Octoberfest Festival. This world-famous event lasts eighteen days, beginning in September and ending on the first Sunday of October. For 2023, it began September 16th and ended October

3rd. This ranks as the largest annual fair in the world, attracting over six million visitors each year. These visitors consume over 2,000,000 gallons of beer and 500,000 half-chickens. Two million gallons of beer translates into twenty-one million 12-ounce bottles of beer. The two "Must have" fair food items are "Fish on a stick" and "Pretzels with cheese."

Publicity for the fair announces it will have beer, food, music, amusement rides, and parades, and admission is free! What else could anyone wish for? There is a very large traveling carnival that provides the Ferris wheel, rollercoaster, etcetera. The major attraction involves the fifteen huge beer tents sponsored by the local breweries. Only beer that is brewed within the Munich city limits is allowed to be served at the fair. It has an alcohol content of 5.8 to 6.3% and is designated Octoberfest beer. A stein of beer, one liter, or 34 ounces, costs about ten dollars. Remember to bring cash. Plastic is not accepted at the fair. The 15 large tents are really big, holding from eight to ten thousand visitors each. There is no admission charge, and the tents are filled with tables and chairs, serving stations, and a performance stage. Each tent has its own special brand of entertainment, a special food menu, and its own special brand of beer. If that's not enough for you, there are about twenty smaller tents accommodating about 500 people each.

One unusual feature specifies an upper sound limit of 82 decibels from 9:00am until 6:00pm to accommodate older visitors and families. The party atmosphere is enhanced by many of the guests wearing traditional German attire, including the famous Bavarian hat with a tuft of goat hair, the women in their Dirndl skirts, and the men in their Lederhosen. An additional highlight each day is a different parade to the fairgrounds sponsored by one of the major breweries and featuring their collection of horse-drawn, vintage beer wagons with marching bands and performing animals.

The original Octoberfest dates to October 1810, when crowds were invited to a meadow in the center of Munich to celebrate the wedding of Prince Ludwig of Bavaria and Teresa of Saxony. It became an annual autumn event, featured horse races, and showcased agricultural products. It wasn't until 1896 that local merchants, working with several of the city breweries, created the first large beer tent, and the festival has been about beer ever since. Nowadays, Octoberfest is celebrated in large cities and small towns around the world.

CHAPTER 5

The Paris Ritz Hotel is certainly near the top of the list of the most luxurious hotels in the world. The hotel has three separate bars, and they are certainly on the list of the most expensive drinking spots on the planet.

The Ritz Hotel opened in 1898 at 15 Place Vendome overlooking the Place Vendome in Paris. The hotel has been featured in many novels, including F. Scott Fitzgerald's "Tender Is the Night" and Hemingway's "The Sun Also Rises" and many movie films, including "Love in the Afternoon," 1957 and "How to Steal a Million," 1966.

The Ritz's most famous guest was Coco Chanel, the French designer, and creator of Chanel #5 perfume, the *little black dress*, Chanel suit, and Chanel bag. A famous quote from Coco Chanel states, "Fashion changes, style lasts forever." She was an extraordinary person, born in a *Poor House* and grew up in a Catholic orphanage. Through a series of brilliant decisions and favorable "friendships," she rose to the very top of the fashion world.

Coco Chanel's store was directly across the street from the Ritz, and she maintained a luxurious apartment above the store; however, in 1937, she moved into a suite at the Ritz, and it was her home for the next 34 years. She passed away at the Ritz in 1971 at the age of eighty-seven.

Beginning in 1940, the German Army occupied Paris, and Hermann Goring made the Ritz the headquarters of the Luftwaffe, the German Air Force; he had a very refined desire for the fine things in life. Coco Chanel continued to live at the Ritz and became a very close friend of many of the Nazi officials. At the end of the war in 1945, she was accused of being a spy and a collaborator with the enemy. Her longtime friend, Winston Churchill, intervened, and the investigation ended abruptly.

When the Ritz first opened, men and women were not allowed to gather in bars. The Ritz opened a smaller bar next to the Main Lounge, the " Ladies Bar," and it allowed only women and married couples. Drinks always had a garnish of a flower, and that custom continues to this day. By 1926, rules relaxed, and Earnest Hemingway began to visit the smaller bar along with F. Scott Fitzgerald. By the 1930s, both bars welcomed men and women to mingle. And the party was on!

The "Ladies Bar" became known as the "Petite Bar" since it only had twenty-five seats. This place became very popular with Ernest Hemingway and F Scott Fitzgerald, and the two of them wrote and drank their way through the 1920s at the "Petite Bar." In 1944, Hemingway, a journalist, led a group of American soldiers who were liberating Paris to the Ritz, and they began to liberate the bar. In 1979, The Ritz did a major remodeling and the "Petite Bar" was redecorated and renamed "Hemingway's Bar" in his honor.

Famous people produce famous events. In 1997, Princess Diana and Dodi Al-Fayed had dinner in the Imperial Suite at the Ritz. Then they left for the fatal auto crash in the nearby tunnel.

Colin Field retired in June 2023-- after 30 years bartending at Hemingway's Bar. A book of his experiences is on the way. His favorite customer was Kate Moss, the supermodel. He even named a drink after her, The Kate Moss Sidecar 76.

The following info is for all my elite and wealthy readers. The Coco Chanel Suite, #302, is available for lease at the current rate of 18,000 to 28,000 pounds per night. The suite is 2000 square feet and can accommodate three guests. Additional perks included limo service. The Ritz claims to have the world's most expensive drink, the Ritz Sidecar, at $1000 per drink. The recipe includes cognac from the Ritz 1830s collection, Cointreau, and Lemon Juice. A regular Ritz Sidecar costs thirty-eight dollars, and the recipe includes two parts Cognac, one part Cointreau, and one piece of lemon. They're good. But I don't think we need a second round! Current room prices, by the way, are 3000 pounds a night on the weekends and 4000 pounds per night on weekdays.

There is a bar named "Harry's Bar" just about everywhere in the modern world. Harry's New York Bar, located at 5 Rue Daunau in Paris, France, is often listed as "The most famous bar in the world." That is a pretty difficult title to award, but if it isn't the most famous, it is pretty close. It has a competitor for the title every year, and coincidentally, it is named "Harry's Bar" in Venice, Italy, and also a famed watering hole for Venetians and tourists alike.

The history of Harry's New York bar is fascinating. The bar was acquired by a star New York jockey, Ted Sloan, in 1911. Sloan's idea was to make the bar a special hangout for all the American artistic and literary folks who were flocking to Paris at the time, using his jockey fame as the attraction. So, Sloan converted a bistro into a bar. And even had a bar from a saloon in

New York City shipped to Paris and installed in the place. He also hired a bartender, Harry McElhone, from Dundee, Scotland, to run the bar and named it the "New York Bar." It is claimed to be the first cocktail bar in Europe.

The bar did become a popular place for Americans, especially those serving in the American Ambulance Corps in the First World War. Unfortunately for Sloan, financial problems resulting from a lavish personal lifestyle forced him to sell the place.

In 1923, MacElhone, the bartender, purchased the bar, and it became "Harry's New York Bar." MacElhone knew how to run a bar, and he personally turned Harry's into the legendary Parisian landmark that it is today. He owned and ran the place until his death in 1958, when his son, Andrew, took over and managed it until 1989. This place has stayed in the family as a grandson, Duncan, took over in' 89 and ran it until 1998. Now, his widow, Isabel MacElhone, has taken over.

The list of Americans who called Harry's home is like a celebrity list from the thirties through the fifties. Knute Rockne, F Scott Fitzgerald, Sinclair Lewis, Humphrey Bogart, and Jack Dempsey. Ernest Hemingway is also included, but he seemed to be in just about every bar in the civilized world. Rita Hayworth and Ali Khan could certainly go anywhere, but Harry's was their favorite.

Harry's conducts a "Straw Poll" before each U.S. presidential election; only customers with proof of US citizenship are allowed to vote in the poll. The results have been absolutely correct, except on three occasions, in 1976, 2004, and 2016, since the poll began in 1924. That's correct in twenty-one out of twenty-four elections over a span of almost 100 years.

The special story about Harry's New York bar includes George Gershwin. Harry's has two levels. The lower level has a piano bar called *Ivories*, and there has always been a dark, mahogany-colored piano in the corner. It was at this piano in the autumn of 1928 that George Gershwin composed the rhapsody

"An American in Paris" inspired by the sights and sounds of the French capital.

Harry MacElhone, in the early years of the bar, began a special, secret, invitation-only club of patrons named "The International Society of Fireflies" dedicated to the art of drinking. The members have small tie clips displaying two handsome men shaking hands. The Club continues to operate today.

Harry's is also known as the origin of some famous drinks: "Sidecar," "French 75", "White Lily," and more.

Today, you can go down this Paris side street, Rue Daunau, between Avenue de l' Opera and Rue de la Paris. The neon sign out front identifies *Harry's*. It's still a friendly neighborhood bar. Step into the softly lit piano bar, velvet-covered booths, candles on the tables, walls covered with black and white autographed photos of guests and pennants of American universities. A trio is in the corner playing jazz. You have taken a step back into the 1930s. James Bond is liable to arrive any minute and order a dry martini; he appears at Harry's frequently in Ian Fleming's novels. What a way to spend the night in Paris, open till 2:00 am.

CHAPTER 6

The Raffles Long Bar, located in the Raffles Hotel, has been famous around the world for over 120 years. It has been mentioned or played a role in many novels and appeared in countless paintings and movies. The hotel opened in 1887, owned by two Americans, the Sarkis brothers, and named for Thomas Raffles, the founder of modern Singapore. From the beginning, the hotel has the look of British colonial architecture. Singapore became a thriving British colony at the beginning of the twentieth century. The export trade of rubber and tin made it one of the busiest ports in the world.

The Raffles Hotel and the bar were at their peak at the turn of the 19th century, 1900. The bar was "the place," and wealthy planters and merchants gathered at the Long Bar to drink gin and whiskey, entertain, and conduct business. Malaysian etiquette at the time forbade women from drinking alcohol in public. In 1915, an enterprising bartender at Raffles named Jim Boone came up with a fruit juice-appearing drink using gin, pineapple juice, lime juice, Curacao, Benedictine, and a touch of Grenadine or cherry juice for a pink color. The drink appeared to be another fruit juice cocktail, and it became an instant hit with the ladies. The "Singapore Sling" was born. The drink became vogueish around the world, especially during the 1950s to 1970s, with the popularity of anything Polynesian. It is still the national drink in Singapore. With all the ingredients and time to prepare, you might correctly expect the Singapore Sling to be expensive. Raffles charges thirty-eight dollars per drink, that's about twenty-eight dollars in US currency.

At the beginning of World War II, 1940, the Japanese bombed Singapore and sunk two Royal Navy battleships, the Prince of Wales, and the Repulse, in one of Winston Churchill's darkest moments. The Japanese occupied Singapore beginning in February 1942, and the British Navy reclaimed it in 1945 and proudly raised the Union Jack on the top of the Raffles Hotel. The Singapore government declared Raffles a National Monument in 1987. The Raffles Hotel even has its own museum displaying photos, past menus, postcards, glass and china, and some rare editions of many of the famous writer's books who sat at the Raffles bar.

The Long Bar at Raffles has served a list of famous guests, especially writers. The list includes W Somerset Maugham, the British author who used to sit in the Palm Court mornings and write stories about the gossip and scandal he had overheard at the Long Bar the night before. Other guests have included the rich and acclaimed; James Michener, Pulitzer Prize-winning author, stayed so many times at Raffles that there is a suite named in his honor. Others who came for extended stays include Charlie Chaplin, Noël Coward, Ava Gardner, and Elizabeth Taylor in the 1950s. Several books have been written about the hotel, the bar, and the many famous guests. Numerous movies have been filmed at Raffles, and it continues to appear in films and TV shows.

The hotel has undergone many major renovations over the past 120 years. Today, all 115 rooms are suites, and prices range from $1300 and up per night. Both inside and out, the place continues to exhibit the old British Colonial Class. There is an adjacent arcade with about 65 boutique shops, including the museum. The latest restoration has restored this "Grand Dame" of the world's luxury hotels to its 1915 elegance, updated with all the modern conveniences.

The Long Bar has always had a tradition of customers eating peanuts and tossing the empty shells on the floor. This tradition is special because it is definitely the only place in Singapore that encourages littering. Singapore is noted for its extremely strict rules regarding littering or damaging the appearance of the city in any way. The city-state continues to be a thriving, independent commercial hub with a growing population of over six million. Singapore currently has the highest per capita gross domestic product in Asia and the highest rent cost index in the world. The Long Bar opens daily at noon.

CHAPTER 7

Harry's Bar in Paris is often considered the world's most famous bar. Harry's bar in Venice, Italy, is also very well known. Harry's Bar is actually a restaurant opened in 1931 by Giuseppe Cipriani. The true story behind the bar involves a wealthy young American named Harry Pickering. Pickering had been living abroad for quite some time, enjoying the good life and spending the family's money. Pickering's main hangout was the Hotel Europe in Venice, where Cipriani was the head bartender. One day, Pickering came in and explained to Cipriani that he wouldn't be around anymore because his family had found out about his lifestyle and heavy drinking and cut him off financially. Cipriani liked Pickering and loaned him 10,000 lire to get back to America, about $8000 in today's US money. Cipriani never heard from Pickering again-- until two years later, he walked into the Hotel Europe and handed Cipriani 50,000 lire. Pickering explained his trust fund had kicked in, and he was wealthy once again. The 50,000 lire included 10,000 to repay the loan and 40,000 to open a bar that they would call "Harry's."

Cipriani was a genius at running a bar. Harry's cultivated the upper-crust crowd, and it worked to absolute perfection. The customers weren't just famous. They were also wealthy: the

Rothschilds, the Prince and Princess of Greece, Arturo Toscanini, Maria Callas, Aristotle Onassis, Barbara Hutton, and Peggy Guggenheim. Once again, Ernest Hemingway was spending a lot of time where the action was taking place. This time, he spent the winter of 1949-1950 drinking and writing at a corner table in Harry's bar.

Cipriani is credited with creating the "Bellini" cocktail, which became quite prominent. The Bellini cocktail is made with fresh white pear juice and Prosecco. The drink is named for the famous fifteenth century Tuscan artist.

Harry's Bar is also well known for its special martinis served in a short glass without a stem. Harry's version of the Montgomery martini is a ratio of gin to vermouth of 10 to one. This was Hemingway's favorite drink at Harry's. It was at the corner table that Hemingway wrote the major portion of the novel "Across the River and Into the Trees."

Cipriani had a special skill for treating his customers. He advised his son to develop friendships with the bar's guests but to always maintain a "polite detachment." The one exception Cipriani made to this rule was Ernest Hemingway.

In 2001, the Italian Ministry of Cultural Affairs declared Harry's Bar a National Landmark, a very prestigious Italian award. Cipriani's incorporated and has grown into an international brand with food and beverage operations around the world, particularly in the US and Argentina, as well as Italy.

An American was having a late supper at a bar in Madrid. The waiter brought a delicious-smelling entree to the couple sitting next to him. The American said to the waiter, "That looks and smells great. What are they having?." The waiter says, "Oh, senior, those are the specialty of the house, bull testicles from the bull ring down at the corner." The American, a little surprised, "Never had those, but I'll try them the next time." The waiter says, "I'll place you on the list. You know they're scarce, and they are our specialty, very popular." American arrives at the bar a few nights later, sits down, and orders the specialty of the house: The waiter delivers the plate with plenty of gravy but only two little balls of meat. American says to the waiter, "Hey, you know this is a much smaller serving than the couple had just a few nights ago." The waiter responds, "Oh, you Americans don't understand. Sometimes, the bull wins!"

CHAPTER 8

A Spanish bar had to be included in this story of bars -- Bar Marcella in Barcelona fills the bill. Open in 1820, the business is Barcelona's oldest operating bar, and little has changed in over 200 years. The interior of this place is actually a museum. The guest list is like a "who's who of the art world": Dali, Picasso, Gaudi, and, of course, Hemingway. Comparing Hemingway's drinking spots in Spain is very much like comparing George Washington's sleeping inns in New England.

Bar Marcella has always been associated with the drink "Absinthe," which has always been the preferred drink of the bohemian class of adventurers and was banned around the world for the first half of the 20th century. Known as the "green fairy" for its color and powers, Absinthe is correctly served with a sugar cube, spoon, and mineral water to dissolve the cube into the rather lethal spirit. Absinthe first appeared as an alcoholic drink in France around 1840. It is rather high in alcohol content, 90 to 145 proof, and is supposed to have mystical powers. This made it popular quickly. By 1900, it was the definite drink of choice among artists, writers, and their followers. One ingredient in Absinthe, derived from general wormwood, along with green annis, are the two major products used in producing Absinthe. Thujone is to

Absinthe as caffeine is to coffee. It is the source of its alleged hallucinating powers. Absinthe is legal in the US only if it does not contain Thujone. Absinthe was first banned in the US in 1912. The ban was lifted in 2007 but with the zero Thujone restriction. Almost all other countries have lifted the ban completely, and Spain never had any restrictions on the sale or composition of Absinthe.

So grab yourselves a silver spoon and a special Absinthe glass with the bottom reservoir and head to Bar Marcella around midnight; the place doesn't open until 10:00 pm, closes at 3:00 am, and you will be able to experience Barcelona the way it was 200 years ago. Be careful. The neighborhood hasn't changed much in 200 years. The "ladies of the night" are still loitering around the corner, and the area has the reputation as Barcelona's "red light district." Somehow, this seedy atmosphere just adds to the allure of this centuries-old bar.

PERSONAL STORIES

The following section of this book describes a dozen true personal experiences from my years of participating in the bar scene.

Mike Manuche's Restaurant was a steakhouse and celebrity sports hangout located at 150 W 52nd Street in midtown Manhattan. The Hilton Hotel is located across the street from Manuche's. In the 1970s, the New York Downtown Athletic Club, which sponsors the annual football Heisman Trophy award, decided they needed a larger venue and moved the televised ceremony to the Hilton Hotel ballroom. As a member of the advertising community in New York, my friends and I always attended this major event, which was loaded with sports celebrities.

On this particular December night, the show was over at about 10:30 pm. We decided to "pop in" to Manuche's for a nightcap before each of us caught the train or the bus home to Connecticut, Long Island, or New Jersey. Of course, Manuche's was crowded; it was always crowded, but this night was really packed!

There were about ten of us, and we finished our drinks, and we each drifted off for home. One of the gang, George Medley, decided to use the bathroom before boarding the bus for Summit, New Jersey. The bathroom at Manuche's was located in the basement, not unusual for New York bars and restaurants. Well, George proceeded to fall asleep in the stall on the toilet. It was closing time for the restaurant, and a final "sweep" of the premises failed to reveal George asleep in the stall.

Now, this is a true story!

When George finally woke up in the dark basement restroom, collected himself, and opened the door, he was met by a large, snarling German Shepherd dog. For the remainder of the night, every time George opened the door, the guard dog was waiting for him and did not appear to be wanting to be petted!

Finally, morning arrived, the lights went on, and the kitchen help arrived. The guard dog was gone. The problem was the kitchen help spoke no English, only Spanish. When George made his exit from the restroom at 7:00 am, the workers promptly called the New York City police. Now, everyone knew if there was one extremely important rule in New York City in the 70s, it was "do not get involved in any way with the New York Police Department." Just the appearance of most of them would make the German Shepherd look like your best friend!

Fortunately, George, sober by now and Irish, was able to explain the situation in a convincing manner--it took a while! We were all in our 40s when this incident took place. George went safely home, a full day late; he didn't go to meetings, take medication, or have a "second coming" personality change, but he never had another drop of alcohol.

As a footnote, George had a marvelous voice. He was the solo vocalist singing our national anthem every July 4th at his hometown's celebration. Maybe he should have broken into song when he was confronted by Manuche's kitchen help?

In the 1970s and 80s, I was working as an advertising manager for the Eastman Chemical Division of the Eastman Kodak company. The research lab of Kodak had discovered by accident a powerful adhesive during World War II, cyanoacrylate, commonly known as super glue. Eastman Chemical began marketing the product to the industry as Eastman 910 adhesive in 1958. A company named Loctite, under a license, introduced the product to consumers as "Super Glue" in the 70s. Eastman decided to market the same product, Eastman 910 adhesive, to the consumer market in 1975. That is when our New York advertising department became involved. Now, Super Glue or 910 adhesive is extremely strong. The first promotion we had showed a helicopter lifting a large Ford farm tractor off the ground using a bond made with one drop of adhesive. The advertising agency's first television ad used a lineman for the Minnesota Vikings and later the San Diego Chargers.

Ed White was no ordinary NFL lineman. He was about six-foot-one and weighed 280 pounds. He was known as the strongest guy in the National Football League because he would win the league arm wrestling contest held in Las Vegas each year at the end of the regular season. He was also noted for being able to tear a big city phone book in half. This was quite a feat since the city phone book could be two to three inches thick in the 1970s. Once Ed began to appear in our TV commercials, we also used him to promote the product at dealer luncheons around the country. At these luncheons, in addition to Ed, we usually included several players from the local NFL team. In Saint Louis, one of the guests was Dan Dierdorf. Dan was an All-Pro Cardinal lineman for many years, from 1975 to 1983. He was also a very funny, quick-witted Saint Louis radio announcer. After football retirement, Dan went on to be a successful Monday Night Football announcer for the ABC network.

At one dealer luncheon, everyone was having a lot of fun. Dan Dierdorf had the microphone and began telling everyone about

Ed White being able to tear the Saint Louis phone book in half with his bare hands. Someone appeared, of course, with the Saint Louis phone book, which happened to be extra thick because it contained both the White and Yellow Pages, residential and commercial. Ed took that phone book, well over two inches thick, folded it once, and just ripped it right in half. It was impressive!

Most large trade shows in the '70s, and '80s were held in Chicago because they had the huge McCormick Place exhibit hall and plenty of hotel space. We were exhibiting 910 Adhesive at the annual Housewares Show. Part of the exhibit included White giving away autographed footballs and signed photos of him in his football uniform. One afternoon, the show closed early, and a group of us went to a Rush Street nightclub for a few drinks. At that time, the Rush Street area was the most vibrant entertainment destination in the country.

We were just having a quiet time drinking, discussing the exhibit, etcetera. The maître d,' a small guy in a fancy tuxedo, came over to me and quietly said that our table was located in the bar area and partially in the dining area. Since the dinner hour was beginning, he would like our group to relocate. I said to Ed White, who was sitting next to me, "Ed, hit him." Well, the instant expression on that guy's face was very similar to the one a three-year-old has when he knows he's messed up his pants. All of a sudden, the poor guy was assuring us there was no need to move we could stay as long as we liked. Assuring him, I was only joking and providing a large extra tip calmed things down. He did tell Ed later that he was going to the restroom to make sure he hadn't soiled himself.

Ed White was a great football player, a really good artist, and an all-around wonderful, smart, fine person.

PJ Clark's is an original Irish saloon located in Manhattan at the corner of 3rd Ave and 55th Street. It has been there since 1884. Since it became a tourist attraction many years ago, there are several other locations around New York City, and even one in San Paulo, Brazil. The saloon was established by an Irish immigrant named Duncan, who hired PJ Clark as a bartender. After about ten years, Clark purchased the place and gave it his name. It was a burger and beer place aimed at serving the many Irish laborers who worked in the surrounding area. Clark and his family lived in the upstairs tenement. Four sons were born there over the bar.

The spot became well known as a "holdout" when the owners refused to sell it as part of the development of a forty-seven-story skyscraper that now surrounds the saloon. The "holdout" was known as "David versus Goliath."

Buddy Holly, at age twenty-two, a famous singer, proposed to his wife at PJ's five hours after they met. Clark's advertises, "You can do that here. Just grab a beer." Nat King Cole was a regular and remarked, "Clark's has the "Cadillac of burgers."

The saloon survived Prohibition by making bathtub gin, serving illegal Scotch imported from Canada, and becoming a popular speakeasy. After Prohibition, Clark's began to gain quite a reputation as a celebrity hang-out. Frank Sinatra frequented a lot of New York night spots, but he usually closed PJ Clark's at his table #20. Johnny Mercer, the songwriter, wrote the hit tune "One for My Baby and One for the Road" on a bar napkin sitting in Clark's. For the song line "so set him up Joe," Mercer explained to Clark's bartender Tommy Joyce, "he couldn't find anything to rhyme with Tommy."

In 1945, the Academy Award-winning film *A Lost Weekend*, four awards, starring Ray Milland and Jane Wyman, was filmed at Clark's. Charles Jackson, a regular, wrote the novel that was the basis for the movie. When noise from the 3rd Ave. elevated train became too loud for filming some scenes, a replica of the interior of Clark's was constructed in Hollywood to finish the film shooting.

In the 70s, Jackie Kennedy was a regular Saturday night patron, bringing John Junior and Caroline in for burgers. Jackie's favorite was a hamburger and spinach salad.

Richard Harris, the actor who is now a teetotaler, was famous for having his regular order of six double vodkas.

My personal true story about PJ Clark's involves a friend of mine named Howard, who was a bachelor living in East Orange, NJ, at the time. Howard and a few friends were frequent night-time visitors to PJ Clark's, "regulars." Things were going along normally one evening, sitting at the bar, looking for women, when Howard left his barstool for a quick trip to the bathroom. When he returned, his stool was occupied by an ordinary-looking, middle-aged guy. Howard explained that he had been sitting there, made a quick trip to the bathroom, and would like to have his seat back. The occupant explained the seat was empty when he arrived, and since the bar was full, he was not about to leave. That is probably the moment Howard made his mistake. He grabbed the lowest rung on the barstool for leverage and just dumped the stool's occupant on the bar room floor. When the gentleman got up, there was a pushing and shoving match that soon developed into a session of wrestling on the floor.

This fracas was causing a commotion in the entire bar, at which point the bartender told the boys to settle their problem out front and "helped" the two of them to the door. From that moment on, Howard's recollection of the event is a complete blank. He awoke flat on his back, gazing up at a Third Ave. Street lamp. Witnesses say it was just one punch that did it. The problem was the barstool occupant happened to be a fellow named Charlie Fusari, a retired champion welterweight boxer. Charlie had an official record of 39 knockouts. Howard was the fortieth! We must point out that Howard joined some elite company since Charlie

Fusari had matches with Sugar Ray Robinson, Rocky Graziano, and the great Tippy Larkin. Charlie Fusari is in the New Jersey Boxing Hall of Fame; Howard is retired and living in Florida.

Two CIA spies are scheduled to meet secretly in Mallow, Ireland. The password for the meeting is "Patrick, what a fine day it is, and tomorrow will be even better." The one CIA spy arrives, goes into a pub, and asks the bartender for Patrick Murphy. The bartender says, "Patrick Murphy is a very common name around here. There's Patrick Murphy, the butcher, and there's Patrick Murphy, the tailor. In fact, my name is Patrick Murphy." the CIA guy says, "Patrick, what a fine day it is;" the bartender interrupts "Oh, you're looking for Patrick Murphy, the spy." The Irish have a difficult time keeping a secret!

Guinness beer is the most popular Irish beer around the world. It has a very unique taste due to the use of roasted, unmalted barley. Guinness has been around since 1759, and today, it is more popular than ever. During the 1990s, Guinness had an annual, worldwide promotion that involved contestants entering a contest by completing an entry form that began with "I like Guinness because" or, in another year, it might begin "the best Guinness I ever had." You had to complete the form in 40 words or less. These entry forms were available everywhere, especially in the Irish pubs of New York City. If you were chosen as a finalist, "the Sweet 16", you were flown to Dublin for the finals. The finals involved a dart-throwing contest and a Guinness beer-pouring contest. Because of the foam generated in pouring a glass full of Guinness, pouring is considered an important step in enjoying the full flavor of the beer.

In 1995, we were living in Little Silver, New Jersey, and my weekend tennis doubles partner was an Irishman named Tom Reardon. Tom's brother-in-law, Frank Gallagher, won the Guinness contest. Frank, at the time, was a sales vice president with Bacardi Rum in Coral Gables, Florida. The annual contest prize was your choice: $250,000 or a real, live, operating pub in Ireland. Frank was 65 years old and about to retire from Bacardi-- he chose the pub. After doing all the necessary publicity chores, appearing on the Today show, and touring around the country visiting Irish pubs, Frank and his wife, June, arrived at their very own Irish pub, "the Kilgoban" in Bantry, Ireland. Bantry is a village of about 3000 on the coast west of Cork City. The pub was pretty large, with two bars and an upstairs apartment with six bedrooms and three bathrooms. June was a wonderful, true Southern lady. We all said this was not going to last very long, moving from Coral Gables, Florida, to Bantry, Ireland, and managing an Irish pub. Well, it lasted 10 absolutely wonderful years. When Frank and June had to sell the pub and return to Florida for health reasons, it was June who really did not want to leave the "emerald isle."

My wife, Babs, and I visited the pub one afternoon and had a special time. Frank had made the place a bit of a sports bar with some large TV sets and lots of photos and sports equipment for decorations. This was a newer concept in Ireland in the 90s, and the Kilgoban became a very successful pub. Frank promised me he was going to write a book about his 10-year adventure, but sadly, he did not have time to do it.

Two Irishmen were drifting in a rowboat in the middle of the ocean when a genie appeared, offering them one wish. Immediately, Patrick shouted, "I wish the whole ocean were a sea of Guinness." And so, it happened. Mike sadly says, "Great, Patrick, now we are going to have to pee in the boat."

In the 1970s, one of Eastman Chemical's major products was a plastic named polypropylene. It was produced at a plant in Texas and shipped all over the world in pellet form for use in molded items or as plastic film or sheeting for packaging.

At about this time, it was found that polypropylene could be used to make a very strong twine, string or rope. Eastman did not normally produce manufactured end-products. We produced and sold only the basic raw materials used to produce the finished items. This time was different, and the company entered not just the rope and string market but the specialty baler twine market. Traditionally, hay was baled using hemp or jute imported primarily from Mexico. Transporting hay was expensive, so bales had become larger and heavier, and wire was replacing hemp as the choice for holding the bales together.

Promoting the advantages of polypropylene baler twine to the agricultural market, especially the California market, was a whole new experience for our New York advertising group. All of a sudden, we were producing billboards with photos of cows, radio "spots" with one-minute commercials, and space ads for agricultural magazines. And, once a year, we exhibited with our distributor in the "Tulare Farm Show," the largest annual outdoor agricultural show in the world. The show continues to be held every year in Tulare, California, it is now known as the "World Ag Expo," with 1500 exhibits and 26,000,000 square feet of exhibit space, attracting 100,000 visitors.

The Eastman exhibit in the first year consisted of a larger-than-life talking cow. The cow was very large, and its mouth opened and closed. We had a very witty announcer with a microphone to comment on the passersby and occasionally on the baler twine.

His favorite act would happen when a small group of teenage farm boys would be examining the cow and innocently wind up gathered behind the cow. That is when using the loudspeaker, the announcer would ask the teenagers to "please step away from the rear of the cow. You can see you're beginning to make her nervous." These young guys would be so embarrassed they would actually flee the exhibit. We used the "talking cow" for several years, and it became closely associated with our brand of twine, "WR 180." This stood for wire replacement, tensile strength of 180 pounds.

After about a year of promoting this product, we produced an ad showing a bale of hay standing in a field of hay. The headline was "WR180 outstanding in its field." Well, it turned out we had used hay instead of alfalfa, which had replaced hay in the California ag market. It was decided the New York ad group needed to know more about baling hay in California. So, I went out there for some farmer education.

The first lesson involved baling alfalfa, which took place at night between 1:00 am and sunup. The timing was due to the days being so hot the bales were so dry they would not hold together. For a guy from Manhattan, this was a very long night! The primetime event occurred when we went to a rural, really rural, saloon for breakfast at sunrise. First, I noticed it had no doors, just those swinging, off-the-floor doors straight out of an old Western movie. Inside, it is now about 6:00 am., the jukebox is playing, a few couples are dancing, others are shooting pool, and the long bar is packed, and people are drinking. We had been working all night. My good friend, our local representative, was a big guy who repaired farm machinery: balers and tractors; he turned to me and said, "Terry, do not make eye contact with any of these women; you will never know what hit you." I had to keep looking down at the floor throughout breakfast. This is the only time I ever had a bourbon for breakfast with fried eggs. I returned there many times, and it remains in my memory as the toughest-looking saloon I've ever seen!

Briody's Irish Tavern was located at 132 E River Road in Rumson, NJ, only about three miles from our home in Little Silver, New Jersey. Rumson is an upscale New York City commuter town with a population of around 7000. Briody's was opened in 1970 by two Irish brothers whose family had owned a bar in Jersey City for many years. It was situated on the corner in a residential area, which made it a neighborhood bar. Briody's was everything a neighborhood bar should be. It was a comfortable place, a place to celebrate birthdays, anniversaries, promotions, graduations, and baby showers; your friends were always there. On Saturdays, it was college football and music in the evening, and on Sunday, the Jets played the Giants.

We celebrated every holiday; Halloween, Christmas, Valentine's Day, and of course, the "big one," Saint Patrick's Day, March 17th. It was after closing on Saint Patrick's Day one year that one of the regulars took his wife home strapped to the ski rack on the top of their station wagon! There were sad times, too. When one of the regulars passed away, his barstool was leaned up against the bar as a gesture, and no one sat there for a week. When the funeral procession passed the saloon on the way to the cemetery, the hearse always stopped out front for a few moments before continuing its sad journey.

Briody's had a special men's club named the "Briody Bunch." Membership was limited to 38 men. My wife and I had been regular customers at Briody's for quite a while before I found out the Club existed. In fact, it was my wife who first heard about the "exclusive club" from an employee at her business. The Club was organized and run by Neil Briody, one of the brothers. It had rules, bylaws, and officers, but the important thing was its sole purpose was to have a good time. Even the meetings were fun since they were held in a room at the saloon with plenty of drinking available. Although the Club was "men only," women were invited to all the parties, trips, and events, which were many!

Jack Connolly was a mainstay at Briody's Saloon. He had his own stool at the front corner of the bar. You may wonder how he could reserve a stool at a busy bar. Well, it was because he was pretty much sitting on it all the time.

Jack was in his 60s, retired, and a fairly big, tough kid from South Buffalo. He owned a business that fit him quite well, the hazardous demolition business. His company specializes in dismantling refineries and chemical plants. Following high school, Jack enrolled in a small college in the Buffalo area and had a football scholarship. After two years, Saint Bonaventure discontinued the football program, and Jack discontinued college. When we first met at Briody's, he was married and had two adult daughters. Something changed in Jack's personal life, and he began spending a lot of time with a woman he had no business spending any time with. A divorce followed, and he wound up marrying his new friend. As we all knew would happen, this marriage lasted less than a year. Which helps explain why Jack was a regular at the end of the bar. He was a wonderful, generous, and very interesting guy. Lots of stories to tell about the demolition business.

One evening, my wife and I took our seats at the busy bar, and Peggy was tending bar, the wife of the owner's son. Peggy came over, and sort of whispered to us, "Jack found out today he has terminal cancer." I felt like someone had just hit me! The place was very busy, but I had to go over and speak with him. Jack told me the details and that he had a niece in Boston, and both she and her husband were medical doctors. Jack said he had arranged to go up there next week for a second opinion.

The second opinion was not good and gave him six to eight months to live. For the next month, Jack continued to come into the bar. He could walk over easily from his apartment. Then the surprise arrived in our mail--an invitation to a celebration of Jack's life to be held on a Saturday evening at Briody's. The party was being organized by his first wife, Mary, who had arranged to "take over" the saloon for the night.

When our bar crowd received this invitation, it sparked a lot of conversation and a few questions. No one had ever been invited to a "celebration of life" party for a person who only had a few months to live. Do we bring gifts? What could possibly be an appropriate gift? We arrived around 6:00, and the place was already crowded. This is noteworthy and a real compliment to Jack and his ex-wife; of all the people invited, every single one replied that they would be there. Two relatives came from San Diego, and there were several friends from the Chicago area.

One of the first things we noticed was the many young people in the crowd. Around 7:00, a band arrived and began playing a little soft background music. Jack was seated at a special table with lots of hometown Buffalo decorations. His parish priest was also at the table along with his two daughters, ex-wife and his brother and his family. Following dinner, gifts were opened, and there were funny ones, clever ones, and a few "nice" ones. We gave Jack a gift he just loved, a mounted large poster depicting the bars of Elmwood Ave., which was always Buffalo's prime entertainment street, like Rush Street in Chicago.

Now, as I mentioned, there were an awful lot of people at the party, and a surprising number of young folks and drinks were "on the House." By 9:00, the atmosphere of the crowd had totally changed from somber to a really full-blown, fun party. The young people, fueled by youth and alcohol, were everywhere and dancing "up a storm." We sat with Mary and Jack and the priest, and we were all smiling. It was everything Mary had hoped it would be. Another night and another reason Irish pubs have been so popular for over 200 years!

Jack passed away a few months later. His two daughters spoke at the reception following the service. The older one spoke first and handled all the humor, and the younger one finished with comments on the serious side. I still believe it was the best eulogy I've ever heard.

When I was transferred to the home office in the 1960s, Kingsport, Tennessee, was a "dry town" in a "dry county." Drinking was only permitted in private clubs, and you had to furnish your own bottle. Pretty much all the business folks and company management belonged to a couple of local clubs. I decided to join the Elks Lodge, which was large and had an impressive building with a lounge and bar, known as the Cypress room because of the wood paneling. The Moose Lodge, which was located just across the road, was even larger and had a big indoor swimming facility. These clubs were not desperate for members, and you needed a sponsor. It was necessary to complete a lengthy application followed by an interview. Following acceptance, an indoctrination course was provided so you would be familiar with the history of the Elks Lodge, its traditions, and its many benefits and charities. After being a member for about six months, I decided to sponsor a couple of my friends. I invited them to attend the upcoming Elks costume Halloween party. This was a big event, several 100 people, held in the main dining room, which had a large stage for bands and entertainment. The other two couples came to our house for a little "front-loading," and I noticed Bob, who happened to be a very talented artist, was not wearing a shirt. He had managed to paint his entire torso with a collection of rather risqué Halloween scenes. Since this covered both front and back, I assumed his son, also, a really good artist assisted with the work. His only upper garment was a small leather vest. No doubt this was extremely clever, but I had some concerns about how this was going to be received by the Elk's membership. Let's say the reaction upon our arrival was "mixed."

Bringing your own booze to a big party usually leads to excess consumption of alcohol by almost everyone. There is no need to go to the bar, there's no need to buy drinks, and no one is measuring the amount.

After a couple of hours of dining, dancing, and drinking, it was close to 11pm. The worldwide Elks Lodge has a very solemn, time-honored tradition known as "Elevens." At 11pm at every single lodge, if a function is being held at 11pm, everything stops to observe a brief period of silence in honor of "absent Elks," and a bell is tolled eleven times. Unfortunately, it was at this serious moment that my two friends decided to appear on stage in their costumes and perform a little skit, which they obviously thought was hilarious. Let me tell you, they were the only ones-- there was only absolute total silence in the room.

This stunt sort of brought the party to a close, but our problems weren't quite over. The six of us, Bob and wife Mary, Marvin and wife Beverly, Babs and me, were standing in the parking lot discussing the "faux pas" of the evening and how lucky we were that most people didn't know us. The parking lot bordered a steep embankment that led down to a stream. Beverly, Marvin's wife, took one step backwards, went down in a heap, and began to roll down the bank. It is surprising how she just kept rolling because it was covered with leaves and underbrush. Beverly wound up at the very edge of the creek, not a river, thank God, but a good-sized creek. Of course, we all had to make our way down to help her out. One more time: "God does protect fools, drunks, and babies." No serious damage, just covered with leaves, twigs, mud, and scratched from head to toe. Upon arriving home and being greeted by the teenage babysitter, who said looking at me, "What happened?" I said, "We had to help a lady up the creek bank at the Elks Club." She wisely replied, "Oh."

Later in the week, I was notified that my friends, Bob and Marvin, applications were being returned.

The Kitty Hawk Bar was located on Madison Ave. near the corner of 42nd Street, across from Grand Central Terminal. The charter buses from La Guardia airport boarded passengers out front. The place had been a retail store and had two very large windows facing the street. The inside motif celebrated everything about flying; model airplanes hung from the ceiling, propellers adorned the walls, and photos of planes everywhere.

Several of our group were having a drink there prior to attending a Knicks game at nearby Madison Square Garden. In walks Ron D., one of our group and a neighbor of mine in New Jersey. It was raining, and Ron had a new golf umbrella. It's not the ideal size umbrella to use in a city, but golf umbrellas were favored promotional giveaways in the 70s and 80s, and we all had several.

After another round of drinks, the group, as we often did, began recalling events that occurred during our days in the military. Ron stood up and, using his umbrella as a prop, began to demonstrate what is called the "manual of arms." Encouraged by the reception his "manual of arms" received and another drink, Ron decided on one more demo, a drill team exercise called "spin arms." A golf umbrella has a handle at one end and a spike about two inches long on the opposite end. The spin arms drill consists of grabbing the rifle near the center with the left hand and using the right hand to grab the barrel and spin the weapon--holding on with the left hand. This is what Ron did, except he lost his grip, and that golf umbrella went spinning through the air across the bar room and stuck near the center of that nine-foot by twelve-foot picture window. There was total silence, and nothing happened for a few seconds. Then, that window slowly became a top-to-bottom, side-to-side spider web.

The following five or ten minutes were not good! Breaking a window in midtown Manhattan, a picture window, in a bar, at 7 in the evening is expensive. In fact, you might as well have scheduled brain surgery.

A company had to come out and board the window up until the glass repair could be done the next day. Fortunately, Kitty Hawk's insurance covered the entire episode, but our group was asked politely to please not come there again.

Fort McClellan, Alabama, is over 100 years old and located adjacent to Anniston, Alabama. It's a large place, over 100,000 acres, and over the years, it has trained hundreds of thousands of U.S. soldiers for service in both world wars and almost every other conflict. It even had a German POW camp located there in 1943. In 1951, the Chemical Corps branch of the Army established its training center and school at Fort McClellan, and this was followed in 1952 by the Women's Army Corps, WAC, moving its headquarters and basic training facilities to the Fort.

The place was not a resort by any stretch, but it had some first-class facilities, including the Officer's Club. This was not unusual for U.S. military operations. Fort Monmouth, the Army Signal Corps headquarters, located in Oceanport, New Jersey, near my hometown of Little Silver, New Jersey, had a wonderful Officer's Club that included a huge bar, ballroom, and an 18-hole golf course. The Fort McClellan Officer's Club had a great outdoor pool, lots of recreational activities, and a very nice bar. The club was in very good financial condition, with over $150,000 in the treasury. This money was entirely the result of the regular Wednesday evening bingo games profit, and it was continuing to grow nicely.

The bar was rectangular in shape and held a nice crowd, probably 40 or more. Friday afternoon was "happy hour," and drinks were half-price. They were already cheap, so a martini on Friday cost $0.25. We all kept telling each other, "We couldn't afford not to drink because the more we drank, the more we saved, and soon we would be able to buy a new car."

A WAC Officer named Dorothy was a regular at the bar. She was a little older, attractive, regular army career person, a captain, and she usually smoked a small cigar. When she wasn't around, I called her Dorothy.

Well, Captain Dorothy was sitting directly across the bar from our little group of about six Second Lieutenants. We were all classmates attending the six-month basic course in chemical, biological, and radioactive warfare. We were all young R.O.T.C. college grads.

Captain Dorothy was soon joined by several of her buddies, and she shouted across the bar, "hey, Lieutenant Lyons, you want to have a little drinking contest?" This was a new and friendly twist. We had all been in the bar many times, and this offer never happened before.

There was no way we could possibly refuse to join a drinking contest challenged by a group of WACS. I, of course, answered, "Sure, Captain." She says, "OK, we'll start with three 10-minute rounds. Marie will keep the time. First one that falls off the stool, that team pays for the drinks."

I will have to say, in our defense, we were at a disadvantage since we had a slight head start with the drinking, and because it was Friday "happy hour," some of us were drinking Martinis and

Manhattans, not just beer or gin -and- tonic. By now, the place was full, a lot of higher-ranking officers and their wives. At the close of the second round, I noticed Bob, actually the largest guy on our team, had become unusually loud and outgoing. Also, he wasn't quite sitting completely on the barstool. Just as we entered round three, Bob did a slow roll off the stool and onto the floor. A loud cheer and plenty of laughter erupted from the opposite side of the bar.

Bob, fortunately, was OK, embarrassed, but OK. In fact, we were all embarrassed. It's not a good thing to happen before a crowd in the Officer's Club-- downtown would have been a much better location. The worst part was the humiliation of having to congratulate Captain Dorothy and her group in front of an audience.

We were stationed there for several more months, and there was never a repeat contest; however, there were onlookers who apparently decided to never let us forget about it.

There is so much publicity these days concerning gun violence in this Country I decided to include a few true stories about my own encounters with bars and pistols. Thankfully, these tales did not involve the tragedy that occurs today with automatic weapons, AK-15s, often in the hands of mentally unbalanced individuals, and the resulting tragedy. We even have a definition now for mass murder, including four or more fatalities.

My first story occurred on a business trip from New York, where I worked, to the home office in Kingsport, TN. I was an advertising manager for the Plastics Division of Eastman Kodak, and we used a large advertising agency located in mid-town Manhattan, J. Walter Thompson. Representatives from the agency and I made frequent trips to Kingsport to discuss advertising strategy and proposals, and I had lived there previously for over five years.

Kingsport is a city of about 35,000, and Eastman Chemical employed about 15,000 at the time, 1970s, it was a company town. As I mentioned previously, it was also a "dry town." Booze was only available in private clubs, the Ridgefield's Country Club, the Elks Club, the Moose Club, and others.

Several folks from the agency and I were on one of our trips. As usual it included meetings all day at the plant, followed by cocktails and dinner at the local country club. As often happens at these gatherings, it seemed to get late awfully fast. Arriving back at the motel, we were flying back to New York in the morning. One of our group had what seemed at the time a brilliant idea, an illegal bar had opened and they probably stayed open longer than the Country Club. Off we went to the Creekside, so named because it was situated on a small creek. You had to park your car and take a footbridge to reach the entrance. Maybe the idea was this would discourage the sheriff if they ever decided to raid the place for illegally serving alcohol. Actually, the police did raid various illegal places for gambling or alcohol, but only once every few years, right before the elections.

Upon entering the Creekside, we immediately realized we were totally "out of place." Four guys from New York dressed in suits and ties while the rest of the bar looked like they had just returned from a four-day hunting trip. The young women appeared about like you would expect! Everyone was drinking the same thing: Tennessee moonshine, which I assure you bore no resemblance to Tennessee Jack Daniels whiskey.

After a round or two of drinking, the bartender/ owner announced the place was closing in ten minutes and everyone should "drink up." One of our group, in a definite New York accented tone, replied back to the bartender, "We were not ready to leave and needed one more round." There was total silence for a moment, and you just knew a mistake had been made. That is when the bartender produced a six-shooter similar in size to the ones used on the TV show "Gunsmoke." Standing behind the bar with that pistol, the bartender, in a very loud voice, said, "One last time-- this bar is closing in five minutes, and anyone who has trouble understanding that I'm here to help them." Considering how much we had to drink, you have to give the four of us credit for the speed with which we exited that bar, crossed that footbridge, and drove out of there. I still remember one of the group, safely in the car, saying, "I think the bastard would have shot us."

One of our largest customers had their research facility and purchasing department located in Terre Haute, Indiana, and I made frequent trips there. There were not a lot of choices, and I always stayed downtown at a motel that had a very busy bar and restaurant.

On one regular visit, I checked into the place, went to my room, watched TV, and returned to the bar for a drink and dinner. The place was very, very busy, so I took a chair at a high-top table in the bar area.

At this point, I need to give a little background information. The time was December 1989, and one of the well-known baseball personalities was Billy Martin. Billy grew up in a rough and tough area of Oakland, California, and he was a very good baseball player. He played second base for the New York Yankees during their best years when Casey Stengle was the manager. Casey treated Billy Martin like the son he never had. Martin's best friend was Mickey Mantle, the star of the team. These two guys were young and very good players having fun in New York City. One day, they would be headlined in the morning newspapers with some special performance on the baseball field, and the next day, the feature would cover their exploits at the Copacabana or some other Manhattan night spot.

Martin seemed to have a special attraction for drinking and fighting. Eventually, Billy became the manager of the Yankees. In fact, he was manager of the Yankees on five separate occasions. The problem was George Steinbrenner was the owner of the team. Unlike most owners, he was very involved in running the club and had a personality similar to Billy. The two of them had a love-hate relationship all the way to the finish line. By 1989, Martin had moved to an administrative job with the Yankees, but at sixty-one years old, he was still looking for a manager's role somewhere.

Now, returning to the bar at the motel in Terra Haute, Indiana. The waitress came by the table and asked me if I was superstitious, and I said, "Sometimes." "Well," she said, "you're sitting where Billy Martin was almost shot last week. No one has sat there since." Now I understood why it was the only seat available.

As she described the story, Billy had come to town to speak at a fundraiser for his good friend, basketball star Larry Bird, at Larry's alma mater, Indiana State. After the dinner and the speech, they returned to the motel, which was owned by Larry. Four of them were sitting at this very same high-top table when a young woman at a nearby table accidentally knocked her girlfriend's purse off the table. When the purse hit the floor, the tiny two-shot derringer in the purse fired the bullet that missed Billy Martin's head by a hair. No charges were filed, and no police report was made. The young woman was "estranged" from her husband and had a permit to carry the weapon in Indiana. The waitress said, "Do you still want to sit here?" I said, "I'm not sure. Is that woman in here again tonight?."

The really sad part of this story occurred just two weeks later, on December 25th, Christmas Day, when Billy Martin was killed in a single-car accident near his home in Johnson City, New York, in the Binghamton area.

My family and I lived in Kingsport, TN, from 1966 to 1970. The city is located in Sullivan County, which was a totally "dry" county. This meant there were no liquor stores, no beer or wine in the grocery stores, and no bars or restaurants serving alcoholic drinks. But alcohol could be served in private clubs, The local country club, the Elks Club, the American Legion, etcetera, but you had to bring your own bottle. The only way you could purchase some alcohol to be served at home or at a party was to drive six miles to Gate City, a tiny town just over the border in Virginia. The Virginia liquor stores were state-controlled, so there were plenty of rules for purchasing booze. My wife and I had been born and raised in Western New York state, where the drinking age was eighteen, and booze was readily available. We'd also lived in Buffalo, Rochester, Atlanta, and Chicago; a dry city was a new experience. One of these many regulations placed a limit on how much you could purchase at one time. As you might expect, this required us to make frequent trips to Gate City, known as a "run to Virginia." On Saturday, three neighbors and I decided to make a "run" up there, it was north of Kingsport, purchase some liquor and have lunch and a few drinks at a real bar.

We had a pretty nice time talking about whiskey prices, golf, and business trips when the waitress came over and said in her mountain accent, "You fellows are surely having a good time. Do you realize you're sitting in the same booth where Jim Larson was shot and killed last Saturday night?" "No kidding we replied. I hadn't heard about that." "Oh," she said, pointing at me, "Stand up, and I'll show you. He was just sitting where you are now." I stood up, pointing to the back of the booth. She said, "See where it's discolored? That's from the bleach they used to clean it up. It was a real mess. We had to close, and it was Saturday night." Someone asked what happened and why he got shot? "Well," she said, "it was that Billy Higgins from up in Big Stone Gap; he just came in and shot poor Jim. He's in the county jail now, but he'll get off. He's always been a little crazy."

I was still standing there staring at the back of the booth where I had been sitting. The waitress is asking if we want another drink?

LAST ROUND

Drinking in bars of some sort goes back a long way. The Romans had Tabernas 2000 years ago. It's encouraging to look around my hometown, Vero Beach, Florida, and realize there are still plenty of places to have a drink and a good time. One of the most popular new spots in town, called *Big Shots*, combines drinking, eating, and hitting golf balls from a simulated driving range. You can still enjoy dancing or listening to music on the weekends in several establishments that feature live, local bands. Of course, there are "sports bars" that are crowded on Saturday and Sunday afternoons or when a championship game or match is being televised.

The wonderful corner neighborhood saloon, where the owner lived upstairs, is pretty much gone, mostly because the neighborhood is gone. Even in Ireland and England, the pubs have begun to close at an alarming rate. There are still 40,000 pubs in England, where it's considered a national treasure. Ireland has about 7,000 pubs. Dublin alone has over 700.

The microbrewery and the tap room are the latest drinking spots, and they have been appearing at an amazing rate over the past ten years. There are currently in 2023, over 9,500 craft breweries in the United States. Most of these include drinking on the premises. There are 3,418 brew pubs and 3,833 tap rooms. A brew pub usually offers food and drinks. A tap room only provides alcohol, more of a tasting and sampling environment.

One of our favorite places in Vero Beach is Sean Ryan's Pub. My wife and I usually have dinner at the bar there on Saturday nights. There is a band playing, TV sets are showing whatever sports are available, and a group of regulars gathers at the far end of the bar. The bar is quite large, with about forty-eight seats. Recently, we had an experience that showed you can still hear interesting stories in a bar. A fellow was sitting next to me, having a drink and an appetizer by himself. I said, "Are you visiting, or are you from here?" He answered, "Am I from here? I guess so, six generations. My family started a real estate business here over 100 years ago." I acknowledged that it was a long time. He went on to say, "We live a long time. I just brought my uncle Ed back from a funeral we attended in New York. He is 92 and lives in a nudist colony in Fort Pierce."

Fort Pierce is another shore town about a dozen miles south of Vero. I certainly did not know there was a nudist colony in Fort Pierce, nor, it turns out, did anyone I know have any idea there was a nudist development nearby.

Well, the next ten or fifteen minutes were occupied with listening to stories about visits to Uncle Ed, who, at ninety-two years old has lived there for fifteen years. Just recently, he had picked Ed up, and he was out front of his house, stark naked, trimming the shrubbery with a pair of hedge shears. He said, "My God, Ed, stop that, you could hurt yourself! You know what I mean?" I said, "I understand perfectly."

The point of all this is you just can't get valuable information like this at Publix or your church bowling league!

Bobby's is another sports bar and restaurant that my wife and I visit frequently. Located on Ocean Ave. in Vero Beach, Bobby's opened in 1981, and it is still owned and operated by Bobby McCarthy, who is there every day.

When the Dodger Major League Baseball team conducted spring training in Vero Beach, Bobby's became sort of the Dodger hangout, especially for the management personnel.

One evening, we were sitting at the bar when a "regular" announced he was leaving for home. About five minutes later, Fred was back and said his car was missing. Well, Fred was older, had a few drinks, and was alone, so the bartenders asked for a little more information. They asked questions like if he was sure he hadn't parked across the street or perhaps in the rear. Finally, a bartender took Fred's keys, and a couple of us went out to find the car; a green Jaguar sedan. We just could not believe someone had stolen a car, but we could not find it. Just as we returned to the bar, all set to call the police, the bar phone rang. The guy on the phone, Bill, says, "I'm in my garage, and I've just driven someone else's car home. I used my keys because I'd already been in the house. Well, after determining it was a green Jaguar, we decided he should drive the car back to the bar.

Once things got sorted out, probably a one-in-a-million coincidence, but the keys for Bill's blue Jaguar worked just fine for opening and starting poor Ed's green Jaguar. Just another interesting night at the local bar!

I've included these two recent personal stories to show that the bar continues to be an interesting and entertaining part of living the *good life*.

LIST OF BARS

Algonquin Hotel Bar - New York City

Anchor Bar - Buffalo, NY

Bar Marsella - Barcelona, Spain

Bemelman's Bar - New York City

Billy Bob's - Ft. Worth, TX

Bobby's Restaurant - Vero Beach, FL

Carousel Lounge - New Orleans, LA

Christiana Campbells - Williamsburg, VA

City Tavern - Philadelphia, PA

Connaught Hotel Bar - London, England

Davy Byrnes Pub - Dublin, Ireland

Eagle Pub - Cambridge, England

Fraunces Tavern - New York City

Globe Inn - Dumfries, Scotland

Green Mill - Chicago, IL

Grenadier - London, England

Harry's - Paris, France

Harry's - Venice, Italy

Koniglicher Hirschgarten - Munich, Germany

Hofbrauhaus am Platzl - Munich, Germany

Kilgoban Pub- Bantry, Ireland

King Cole Bar - New York City

Last Chance Saloon - Oakland, CA

McSorley's Saloon - NYC (aka McSorley's Old Ale)

Menger Hotel Bar - San Antonio, TX

Musso and Franks - Los Angeles, CA

My Brothers Bar - Denver, Colorado

Nassau Inn - Princeton, NJ

Oktoberfest - Munich, Germany

Prospect on Whitby - London, England

Old Cheshire Cheese Pub - London, England

Oyster Bar - Boston, MA

Palace Saloon - Prescott, AZ

Pete's - New York City

Pump Room - Chicago, IL

Raffles Hotel Lounge Bar - Singapore

Ritz Hotel Hemingway Bar - Paris, France

Round Robin Bar - Washington, DC

Sean Ryan Pub - Vero Beach, FL

Stonewall Inn - New York City

Stork Club - New York City

Talbots - Bardstown, KY

Temple Bar - Dublin, Ireland

Tootsies Nashville, TN

Top of the Mark - San Francisco, CA

Warren Tavern - Charlestown, MA

Wayside Inn - Sudbury, MA

Sources

Chapter One

"Life Visits the Top of the Mark" July 1944

Top of the Mark, history Intercontinental Hotels

Sloppy Joe's, a Key West Tradition

History of Sloppy Joe's Bar, To discount (9-15-22)

"To Have and Have Not," Ernest Hemingway, 1937 film 1944

"Hamlet the Algonquin Cat" author Leslie Martin

"Algonquin Cat" Dell Schaffner

Hotel History, the Algonquin Hotel 1902 ; hospitality net Stanley Turket

"The Green Mill Essentials" Chicago Tribune, October 22nd, 2013

"The History and Mystery of the Menger Hotel" Republic of Texas Press, 2000

The Menger Hotel - mengerhotel.com

History of Ambassador East Hotel, Chicago Tribune, September 12th, 2023

The Fabulous Pump Room, Gourmet 1963

"Holy Cow," autobiography 1963, Harry Carey

Fort Worth Stockyards newsletter, 2024

King Cole Bar, TripAdvisor

King Cole Bar, Saint Regis hotel, New York Magazine, 2023

The Bemelmans Bar, Gourmet Magazine, December 2022

"Our History" Nassau Inn

Princeton history, Princeton Historical Society

History of Pete's Tavern: on back of menu

Musso and Frank.com

"The Palace Restaurant and Saloon" Fodors, November 15, 2015

Hotel Monteleone.com September 2023

Old Talbot Tavern, tripadvisor.com 2023

"History of Tavern," talbots.com September 1, 2008

Round Robin Bar, washingtonintercontinental.com

"Belly Up Jim Hughes of the Round Robin" Washington, March 13, 2018

unionoysterhouse history.com 2023

Union Oyster House , TripAdvisor. com

"Heinold's First and Last Chance Saloon" National Register of Historic Places
National Park Service

Tootsies Orchid Lounge, Nashville downtown. com

My Brothers Bar, uncovercolorado.com August 2823

bucketlistbars.com August 2023

"The Top 10 Secrets of McSorley's Old Ale House in New York City"

Unstopped New York, August 15th, 2018

"McSorley's Wonderful Saloon" Joseph Mitchell, June 5, 2001

History of McSorley's Old Ale House
McSorley's old ale house in NYC. History August 2003

Warren Tavern.com, history July 2023

National Register of Historic Places January 2007

At Union House, A Feast of History, Boston Globe, August 3, 2011

union oyster house, crayon. Com, September 21, 2017

Travel Chicago come tourist must see sights, travel Sedona. Com Chicago Blues and Jazz

An Oral History of the Green Mill, Chicago Reader, Patrick Sissonne, March 20, 2014

Ohio to California National Park Units

50 shades of gay. com the Seven LGBTBA Wonders of the World

Rise Module: Pride Month usetown.org what we do to educate.

Anchor Bar, Wikipedia

Food Pilgrimage: Buffalo Wings in Buffalo, USA Today, August 1, 2019

Eleven Best Bars in New York City for a Fun Night Out, mybartender.com

Chapter Two

Fraunces Tavern, National Register of Historic Places

Fraunces Tavern, Encyclopedia Americana

U.S. history.org city tavern tour

visitphilly.com citytavern

Christiana Campbell Encyclopedia, Virginia

"Christiana Campbells Tavern" A Taste of Virginia History, John F Blair

Wayside Inn Historic District, National Park Service

"Longfellow, His Life and Work" Newton Arvin 1963 Little, Brown and Company

Find of the Day Stork Club, restaurantingthroughhistory. com

Sherman Billingsley - Wikipedia August 2023

Good Reads, quotes by Lady Nancy Astor

Chapter Three

"Churchill In Quotes" Amanita Press 2018

"Churchill," Roy Jennings, 2001

"The Churchills, In Love and War," Nancy S Lavelle

Historic England The Eagle Inn," National Heritage List for England

London's Most Exclusive Pubs, Frommer's England

Connaught Hotel London official site cosmopolischic.com, a history of the Connaught hotel

Points of interest, Scotland Starts Here

Davy Byrnes, Trip Advisor Travelers Choice 2022

Ulysses, novel, James Joyce

Temple Bar-home page-December 2023

Chapter Four

Munich, Hofbräuhaus and History 2006, Jeffrey S Gaab

Hofbräuhaus official website August 2023

Welcome to Munich Octoberfest 2024, official website

A History. Octoberfest beer festival. com

Beer Tents, theoctoberfestwebsite 2013

Hirshgarten, Munich Trip Advisor 2023

Chapter Five

The Ritz, 2023 Frommer's Paris page 111

A Legend in Progress-- Ritz Magazine September 2013

Harry's New York Bar, Paris Trip Advisor

Harry's New York Bar, official website

Visit Paris. com August 2023

Harry's Bar, Venice Italy, Conde Nast Traveler 2023

Cipriano.com Harry's bar

Chapter Six

www.raffles., June 2023

Raffles Hotel-About Us Fairmont Raffles Hotel 2019

Raffles Hotel-Long Bar, Fairmont Hotels International

Chapter Eight

Bar Marcella (1820) Barcelona Navigator, June 2023

Bar Marcella Wikipedia June 2923

www.ingramcontent.com/pod-product-compliance
Lightning Source LLC
Chambersburg PA
CBHW060852280326
41934CB00007B/1012

* 9 7 8 1 9 7 0 1 5 3 4 8 4 *